Christmas Mosaic

Christmas Mosaic
An Illustrated Book Study for Advent and Christmas

Cay Gibson

With
Mary Ellen Barrett
Margot Davidson
Karen Edmisten
Kathryn Faulkner
Elizabeth Foss
Alice Gunther
Dawn Hanigan
Gwen Wise

Hillside Education
475 Bidwell Hill Road
Lake Ariel, PA 18436

www.hillsideeducation.com

Edited by Rose Decaen and Margot Davidson
Original artwork by Sean Fitzpatrick
Book design and Appendix content by Margot Davidson
Cover design by Stephani Bryson

Recipes in this book were contributed by our readers. These are family traditional recipes and in some cases the source could not be identified. The publisher requests copyright documentation for future printings.

All Scripture quotations are taken from the Catholic Edition of the Revised Standard Version of the Bible, copyright 1965, 1966 by the Division of Christian Education of the National Council of Churches in the United States of America. Used by permission. All rights reserved.

Any other omission of credits is unintentional. The publisher requests documentation for future printings.

Grateful acknowledgement is made to the publishers who granted permission to reprint the picture book covers. Credits listed in order of appearance in this book.

Odds Bodkin/Terry Widener. *The Christmas Cobwebs* (Harcourt, 2001).
Illustrations copyright © Terry Widener, reprinted by permission of
Harcourt, Inc.

Madeleine L'Engle. *The Twenty-four Days Before Christmas* (Random House, 1984).
Copyright©1984 by Crosswicks, Ltd. Illustrations© 1984 by Joe DeVelasco.
Used by permission of WaterBrook Press, a division of Random House.

Susan Wojciechowski/P.J. Pynch. *The Christmas Miracle of Jonathan Toomey*
(Candlewick Press, 1995). Text © 1995 Susan Wojciechowski. Illustrations
©1995 P.J. Lynch. Reproduced by permission of the publisher, Candlewick Press,
Inc. Cambridge, MA.

Elizabeth Winthrop/Bagram Ibatoulline. *The First Christmas Stocking* (Delacorte
Press, 2006). Jacket cover from *The First Christmas Stocking* used by permission
of Random House Children's Books, a division of Random House, Inc.

Patricia Polacco. *An Orange for Frankie* (Philomel, 2004). Reprinted by permission
Of Penguin Group, Inc.

Will Moses. *Silent Night* (Putnam Juvenile, 2002). Reprinted by permission of
Penguin Group, Inc.

Eve Bunting/Ted Rand. *Night Tree* (Harcourt, 1995). Illustrations copyright © Ted
Rand, reprinted by permission of Harcourt, Inc.

Gloria Teles Pushker. *Toby Belfur Never Had a Christmas Tree* (Pelican Publishing
Company, 1991). Reprinted by permission of the publisher, Pelican
Publishing Company.

Gillian McClure. *The Christmas Donkey* (Sunburst, 1995). Reprinted by permission
of Farrar, Strauss, and Giroux.

Geraldine McCaughrean/Fabian Negrin. *Father and Son: A Nativity Story*
(Hyperion, 2006). Reprinted by permission of Hyperion.

Maud Hart Lovelace. *The Trees Kneel at Christmas* (ABDO and Daughters Inc.
Publishing, 1994). Reprinted by permission of ABDO and Daughters Inc.

This book is dedicated to my wonderful parents—Ruel and Gloria Sonnier—who made sure the "visions of sugarplums" that danced in my head came true, and to my brother Vince who shared the sugarplums, the gerbils, the bikes, the cardboard fireplace, and the visions with me. Thank you for your support, your prayers, your love, and for all those joyful Christmases.

—C. G.

Christmas joy is in my heart

Acknowledgements

A book is never written by just one person. The ideas here, the activities, the book selections, the recipes, etc. have all come from people who hold Christmas near and dear to their hearts.

My sincere thanks:

—To editor, Rose Decaen, for seeing each piece she edits as a carol and making the writing sing;

—To my publisher, Margot Davidson, at Hillside Education for sharing the vision and orchestrating the whole Christmas production;

—To artists Sean Fitzpatrick and Stephani Bryson who can hang tinsel with flair;

—To the online communities of Real Learning (www.4reallearning.com) and Literature Alive! (http://groups.yahoo.com/group/LiteratureAlive/) who presented book selections with the grace of the Magi;

—Last, but not least, to my writer friends who contributed articles to this *Mosaic* book and who share with me, all year round, the best present of all…the gift of self:
>Mary Ellen Barrett
>Karen Edmisten
>Kathryn Faulkner
>Elizabeth Foss
>Alice Gunther
>Dawn Hanigan
>Gwen Wise

Note from the Author

Many years ago I was pushing a blond-headed, blue-eyed baby boy through the department store when I overheard a little girl ask her mother, "Mommy, how much longer until Christmas gets here?" The mother, overwhelmed with the shopping task at hand, began to lament the expense and commercialism and over-zealous expectations of Christmas to the little sprite in her shopping cart. The little girl was drawn into her mother's grown-up version of disillusion and disenchantment as her mother ended her tirade with "Christmas comes way too soon, if you ask me!"

I lifted my son's drooling chin and allowed him to slurp on my finger rather than the shopping buggy's germ-infested handlebar; and I made a commitment to myself never to speak disgruntling of Christmas to him, never to be disillusioned by the expense and commercialism, and never to become disenchanted by over-zealous expectations. Each year I would remind myself and my child that Christmas was really just a baby and a family wrapped in the soft heavenly glow of starlight.

Many Christmases have passed since that new mother made that resolve to herself. Many Christmas dinners have been eaten, many presents have been bought and wrapped, and more babies have been added to the Christmas photo greeting. Many times I have faltered (and sometimes failed) in my resolve. This Christmas that little blond-haired, blue-eyed baby boy is a twenty-year-old, six-foot-one man with much darker hair and eyes turned hazel (sometimes they're still blue depending on his mood and what he wears). In Christmases past, his father and I have gone overboard on gifts, have shaken our heads over the commercialism, have worried about the expense, and have faced the disillusionment and disenchantment head-on.

Yet each year there is always some starry night that I bask in a bejeweled Christmas tree a-twinkle with lights and a straw-laden nativity set on a table nearby. I draw back from what the outside world views and any parties and merrymaking that are echoing through the frosty streets that night and I breathe in the Christmas spirit that only quiet and reverie can bring. I remember the wonderment of Christmas that only the very young can wrap their arms around and I recommit to focusing on the baby and family and starlight rather than the expense and the commercialism and unattainable expectations. My belief in and my love for Christmas has not swayed.

Christmas is not what the world makes of it, but what we make of it.

In many ways, *Christmas Mosaic* and the picture books found here will touch the adults more so than the children. The messages and carols found in these books are my Christmas card to all of you who guide these young spirited souls and pray over them and wrap your arms around them in a read-aloud snuggle. These books are my wish to all of you to remember Christmases of long ago and what Christmas is all about, to rejoice in the joy of Christmas and your own families, to focus on the "reason for the season," and to wrap yourself and your children in wonderment on starry, wintry nights in the soft glow of a scented candle and lights upon the Christmas tree.

Table of Contents

Introduction

When you open this book, you might not know where to begin. Like a kitchen island covered with baking ingredients, it is filled with tempting morsels begging you to take a taste. Just like the Christmas season itself, *Christmas Mosaic* appeals to our senses and speaks to our hearts.

What is in this book? You'll have to "peruse the ingredients" to find out. There are illustrated books that tempt your eyes, recipes that tempt your taste buds and sense of smell, poetry that tempts your ears, and crafts that tempt your sense of touch. And that's the beauty and art of picture books; they touch all five of your senses.

So many choices. So much to bake. So many ways to decorate. These books are not your standard cookie-cutter array, but a mosaic of bright, colorful, enriching, and heart-touching books.

This book and the picture books it presents focus on the following categories:

- Holiday Decorating and Preparations
- The Spirit of Giving
- St. Nicholas and Santa Claus
- Family
- Hanukkah
- The Nativity
- Epiphany
- Angels
- Christmas Around the World
- Various Versions of "Twas the Night before Christmas"

Taken together, the morsels in this book make up a feast for you and yours, a mosaic of images and ideas.

Christmas Mosaic represents all the childhood delights, joys, and goodness that we associate with this blessed season. Each story, each activity, in this book feeds your child's heart, mind, and soul in ways that your baked Christmas treats can't. While the Christmas cookie will be eaten and forgotten; the time you spend enjoying this book with your child will last forever.

How to Use this Book

Christmas Mosaic includes study guides for 30 different children's picture books about Christmas (including Advent and Epiphany). Since there are many more books featured than you could use in one year, this resource will be useful for several years. Each year you might select different titles to enjoy, or perhaps your family will have favorites that you return to year after year as part of your Christmas tradition. This book provides you the flexibility of simply sharing the books with your children and enjoying the accompanying activities, or of making a more formal book study. Each study guide, with a few exceptions, includes vocabulary words, discussion questions, a "parent's help page," copywork suggestions, observations, and enrichment activities.

The featured books will be enjoyed by children of ages as well as adults. Many of the books are in print or are available at your local library. Some will have to be purchased used, and some you will want to own in beautiful, lasting, hardback editions. At the end of the booklist, you will find a few blank pages so that you may list other books you discover yourself.

Student Activities for Each Book

Vocabulary Words
Go over the vocabulary words with your child to make sure he/she understands them. Providing oral explanations of the vocabulary words is very helpful. Let the child define the words he/she knows. If there is a word he/she does not know, gently give the definition. When you come across the word in the text, remind your child of the definition. Then with the definition fresh on his/her mind, reread the sentence.

Discussion Questions
The discussion questions are designed to foster conversation between parent and child. After reading the story with your child, ask him/her the discussion questions. Allow your child to answer the questions. Do not attempt to answer the questions for him/her, and do not incorporate a test format into your discussion session. Remember, the questions are intended to be used as conversation starters. (The questions possibly add an extra 5-10 minutes to your reading time.)

Copy Work
This is a special line or phrase from the book which bears repeating and memorizing. At some point, have your child copy the line or phrase into a prayer/reading journal, a copy notebook, or onto the designated activity project. These lines could also be included in the liturgical notebook. (Not every book has a copywork assignment. For those weeks, you might look for a Scripture verse for the child to copy.)

Parent's Help Page

On this page the parent is given more information about the story and activity suggestions to extend the ideas in the story.

Observation
These are suggestions for you to make sure your child practices an objective eye in observing and discerning clues within the story. They may also include special things that the illustrator designed to add richness or extra information to the story.

Discussion Answers
Some suggested answers for the questions are given for the parent.

Enrichment Activities
These are simple and doable activities that reinforce the message found in the story. There is little to no preparation work for the parent. The child may do the activity some time during the week.

Extras for the Parent
Christmas Mosaic also includes a variety of holiday poetry, recipes, and crafts to accompany the stories. There is also a reproducible coloring page section in the Appendix.

Christmas Mosaic Booklist

Christmas Mosaic Booklist

This booklist is as endless as the possibilities for Christmas tree decoration. Even up to the publishing deadline, I was still adding titles. It was as though I was looking at a Christmas tree and no matter which angle I turned it there was a gaping bookless hole, waiting to be filled. There will always be a book that someone treasured as a child that escaped me, and there will be new books published this Christmas . . . and the next.

That tree never stops grinning at me. I finally had to let it go and leave it to you to add your own treasured touches. For this, we have added a few blank pages for you to include your own beloved Christmas books that are not listed here. In that way, you will add the finished touch to your Christmas reading time and make it truly yours.

Bold signifies Pre-School Appropriateness
✳ **Indicates a title featured in *Christmas Mosaic***
OOP Indicates "out-of-print"

Month of December

☐ ***B is for Bethlehem: A Christmas Alphabet*** by Isabel Wilner/ Elisa Kleven
☐ *Christmas in the Stable* by Beverly K. Duncan
☐ *Christmas Cookies: Bite-Size Holiday Lessons* by Amy Krouse Rosental/ Jane Dyer
☐ *S is for Star: A Christmas Alphabet* by Cynthia Furlong Reynolds/ Pam Carroll
☐ *The Advent Book* by Jack and Kathy Stockman
☐ *The Nativity* by Juan Wijngard
☐ ***The Night Before Christmas* by Clement Moore/ Tasha Tudor/ Will Mose**s (or you may choose one of several other illustrated versions)
☐ *The Way to Bethlehem* by Inos Biffi/ Franco Vignazia
☐ *When It Snowed That Night* by Norma Farber/ Petra Mathers (a collection of Christmas poetry)

Advent Week One

Advent/ Decoration/ Preparation Stories
☐ ✳ *Cobweb Christmas* by Shirley Climo/ Jane Manning
☐ ✳ *The Christmas Cobwebs* by Odds Bodkin/ Terry Widener
☐ ✳ *The Cobweb Curtain* by Jenny Koralek/ Pauline Baynes
☐ ✳*The Christmas Miracle of Jonathan Toomey* by Susan Wojciechowski/ P.J. Lynch
☐ *A Christmas like Helen's* by Natalie Kinsey-Warnock/ Mary Azarian
☐ *A Wish to be a Christmas Tree* by Colleen Monroe/ Michael Glenn Monroe
☐ ***Allie, the Christmas Spider* by Shirley Menendez/ Maggie Kneen**
☐ *An Early American Christmas* by Tomie dePaola (OOP)
☐ *Apple Tree Christmas* by Trinka Hakes Noble
☐ *Bear's First Christmas* by Robert Kinerk/ Jim LaMarche
☐ *Christmas Day in the Morning* by Pearl S. Buck/ Mark Buehner
☐ *Christmas in the Country* by Cynthia Rylant/ Diane Goode
☐ ***Christmas Is . . .* by Gail Gibbons**

- ☐ *Christmas on the Farm* by Bob Artley
- ☐ *Christmas Tapestry* by Patricia Polacco
- ☐ **Christmas Tree Farm by Ann Purmell/ Jill Weber**
- ☐ **Christmas Tree Memories by Aliki (OOP)**
- ☐ **Country Angel Christmas by Tomie dePaola**
- ☐ **Deck the Halls by Iris Van Rynbach**
- ☐ *Hanna's Christmas* by Melissa Peterson/ Melissa Iwai
- ☐ **If Christmas Were a Poem by Ronnie Sellers/ Peggy Jo Ackley**
- ☐ *Merry Christmas, Strega Nona* by Tomie dePaola
- ☐ **Mother Hubbard's Christmas by John O'Brien**
- ☐ *One Splendid Tree* by Marilyn Helmer/ Dianne Eastman
- ☐ *Silent Night: The Song and its Story* by Margaret Hodges / Tim Ladwig
- ☐ *The Attic Christmas* by B. G. Hennessy/ Kate Kiesler
- ☐ *The Beautiful Christmas Tree* by Charlotte Zolotow/ Yan Nascimbene
- ☐ *The Cat Who Knew the Meaning of Christmas* by Marion Chapman Gremmels/ Dave LaFleur   (OOP)
- ☐ *The Christmas Witch* by Ilse Plume (OOP)
- ☐ *The Fir Tree* by Hans Christian Andersen
- ☐ *The Legend of the Candy Cane* by Lori Walburg/ James Bernardin
- ☐ *The Legend of the Christmas Tree* by Rick Osborne/ Bill Dodge
- ☐ *The Legend of the Poinsettia* by Tomie dePaola
- ☐ *The Little Christmas Tree* by Karl Ruhmann/ Anne Moller
- ☐ *The Little Match Girl* by Hans Christian Andersen/ Rachel Isadora or other various Illustrators (Study guide found in *Catholic Mosaic*, available at www.hillsideeducation.com).
- ☐ *The Littlest Christmas Tree* by Janie Jasin/ Pam Kurtz
- ☐ *The Nutcracker* (several adaptations and illustrated versions)
- ☐ *The Year of the Perfect Christmas Tree* by Gloria Houston/ Barbara Cooney
- ☐ *Uncle Vova's Tree* by Patricia Polacco
- ☐ *Waiting for Noel* by Ann Dixon/ Mark Graham
- ☐ *When Christmas Came* by Eileen Spinelli/ Wayne Parmenter
- ☐ *Why Christmas Trees Aren't Perfect* by Richard H. Schneider/Elizabeth J. Miles

Advent Week Two

Giving
- ☐ ✻ **The Shoemaker's Dream by Masahiro Kasuya/Mildred Schell**
- ☐ ✻ **A Small Miracle by Peter Collington**
- ☐ ✻ *The Christmas Candle* by Richard Paul Evans/ Jacob Collins
- ☐ ✻ *Why the Chimes Rang* by Raymond MacDonald Alden
- ☐ ✻ *The First Christmas Stocking* by Elizabeth Winthrop/ Bagram Ibatoulline
- ☐ ✻ *The Bears' Christmas Surprise* by Bruno Hachler/ Angela Kehlenbeck
- ☐ ✻ *The Christmas Coat* by Clyde Robert Bulla/ Sylvie Wickstrom (OOP)
- ☐ *A Child's Christmas at St. Nicholas Circle* by Douglas Kaine McKelvey/Thomas
- ☐ *A Christmas Carol* by Charles Dickens, illustrated by Brett Helquist

- ☐ *A Christmas Gift for Mama* by Lauren Thompson/ Jim Burke
- ☐ *A Gift for the Christ Child* by Linda Schlafer/ Anne Wilson
- ☐ *Christmas Eve Blizzard* by Andrea Vlahakis/ Emanuel Schongut
- ☐ *Christmas in the Trenches* by John McCutcheon/ Henri Sorensen
- ☐ *Christmas Moccasins* by Rayn Buckley
- ☐ *Christmas Tree Farm* by Ann Purmell/ Jill Weber
- ☐ *Christmas Soup* by Alice Faye Duncan/ Phyllis Dooley/ Jan Spivey Gilchrist
- ☐ *December* by Eve Bunting/ David Diaz
- ☐ *Good King Wenceslas* by John M. Neale/ Tim Ladwig
- ☐ *Great Joy* by Kate Dicamillo/ Bagram Ibatoulline
- ☐ *Hannah's Bookmobile Christmas* by Sally Derby/ Gabi Swiatkowska
- ☐ **How God Decorates Heaven for Christmas** by Ron Mehl and Melody Carlson/ **Lynn Bredeson**
- ☐ *How the Grinch Stole Christmas* by Dr. Seuss
- ☐ **Jingle the Christmas Clown** by Tomie DePaola
- ☐ *Josie's Gift* by Kathleen Bostrom/ Frank Ordaz
- ☐ *Pages of Music* by Tony Johnston/ Tomie dePaola
- ☐ *Prairie Christmas* by Elizabeth Van Steenwyk/ Ronald Himler
- ☐ *Silver Packages* by Cynthia Rylant/ Chris K. Soentpiet
- ☐ *Stephen's Feast* by Jean Richardson/ Alice Englander
- ☐ *The Candle in the Window* by Grace Johnson/ Mark Elliott
- ☐ *The Christmas Knight* by Jane Louise Curry/ Dyanne DiSalvo-Ryan
- ☐ *The Clown of God* by Tomie dePaola (study guide found in *Catholic Mosaic*, available from www.hillsideeducation.com)
- ☐ *The Elves and the Shoemaker* by the Brother Grimm/ Jim LaMarche
- ☐ *The Gift of the Christmas Cookie* by Dandi Daley Mackall / Deborah Chabran
- ☐ *The Gingerbread Doll* by Susan Tews/ Megan Lloyd
- ☐ *The Give-Away: A Christmas Story* by Ray Buckley
- ☐ *The Legend of the Christmas Stocking* by Rick Osborne/ Jim Griffin
- ☐ *The Light of Christmas* by Richard Paul Evans/ Daniel Craig Kinkade
- ☐ **The Little Drummer Boy** illustrated by **Ezra Jack Keats**
- ☐ **The Twelve Days of Christmas** (various illustrated versions)

Santa Claus
- ☐ ✶ **Santa's Favorite Story** by Hisaka Aoki/Ivan Gantschev
- ☐ *How Christmas Began* by Claire Boudreaux Bateman/ Hannah E. Romero
- ☐ **Santa and the Three Bears** by Dominic Catalano
- ☐ *Santa Comes to Little House* by Laura Ingalls Wilder/ Renee Graef
- ☐ *The Polar Express* by Chris Van Allsburg
- ☐ **Twas the Night before Christmas** by Clement Moore/ various illustrators
- ☐ *Yes, Virginia, There is a Santa Claus* by Francis P. Church/ Joel Spector

St. Nicholas
- ☐ **Can We Help You, St. Nicholas** by Gerda Marie Scheidl/ Jean-Pierre Corderoc'h
- ☐ *Saint Nicholas* by Ann Tompert
- ☐ **Saint Nicholas: The Real Story of the Christmas Legend** by Julie Steigemeyer/

Chris Ellison

- ☐ *The Baker's Dozen* by Heather Forest/ Susan Gaber
- ☐ *The Baker's Dozen: A Saint Nicholas Tale* by Aaron Shepard/ Wendy Edelson
- ☐ *The Legend of Saint Nicholas* by Demi
- ☐ *The Legend of St. Nicholas: A Story of Christmas Giving* by Dandi Daley Mackall/ Guy Porfirio
- ☐ *The Miracle of Saint Nicholas* by Gloria Whelan/ Judith Brown (study guide found in *Catholic Mosaic*, available from www.hillsideeducation.com).

Advent Week Three

Family

- ☐ ✳ *An Orange for Frankie* by Patricia Polacco
- ☐ ✳ *Silent Night* by Will Moses
- ☐ ✳ *The Christmas Promise* by Susan Bartoletti/ David Christiana (OOP)
- ☐ ✳ *One Christmas Dawn* by Candice Ransom/ Peter Fiore (OOP)
- ☐ ✳ **Night Tree by Eve Bunting**
- ☐ *An Alcott Family Christmas* by Alexandra Wallner (OOP)
- ☐ *An Ellis Island Christmas* by Maxinne Rhea Leighton/ Dennis Nolan
- ☐ *Christmas in the Big Woods* by Laura Ingalls Wilder/ Renee Graef
- ☐ *Christmas is Coming* by Anne Bowen/ Tomek Bogacki
- ☐ *Coal Country Christmas* by Elizabeth Ferguson Brown/ Harvey Stevenson
- ☐ *The Farolitos of Christmas* by Rudolfo Anaya
- ☐ *Home for Christmas* by Jan Brett
- ☐ *Irene Jennie and the Christmas Masquerade* by Irene Smalls/ Melodye Rosales
- ☐ *My Prairie Christmas* by Brett Harvey/ Deborah Kogan Ray (OOP)
- ☐ *The Christmas Box* by JoAnne Stewart Wetzel
- ☐ *The Christmas Sweater* by Glenn Beck
- ☐ *The Log Cabin Christmas* by Ellen Howard

Hanukkah

- ☐ ✳ *Toby Belfer Never Had a Christmas Tree* by Gloria Teles Pushker/ Judith Hierstein
- ☐ *Festival of Lights* by Maida Silverman/ Carolyn S. Ewing
- ☐ *Grandma's Latkes* by Malka Drucher/ Eve Chwast (OOP)
- ☐ *Hanukkah at Valley Forge* by Stephen Krensky/ Greg Harlin
- ☐ **Hanukkah Lights, Hanukkah Night by Leslie Kimmelman/John Himmelman**
- ☐ *Hanukkah Moon* by Deborah da Costa/ Gosia Mosz
- ☐ **Hooray for Hanukkah! by Fran Manushkin/ Carolyn Croll**
- ☐ *Just Enough Is Plenty* by Barbara Diamond Golden/ Seymour Chwast
- ☐ *It's a Miracle!: A Hanukkah Storybook* by Stephanie Spinner/ Jill McElmurry
- ☐ *Latkes and Applesauce* by Fran Manushkin/ Robin Spowart
- ☐ *Light the Lights! A Story About Celebrating Hanukkah and Christmas* by Margaret Moorman
- ☐ *Lots of Latkes* by Sandy Lanton/ Vicki Jo Redenbaugh
- ☐ *Moishe's Miracle* by Laura Krauss Melmed/ David Slonim

☐ *Northern Lights* by Diana Cohen Conway/ Shelly O. Haas
☐ *One Candle* by Eve Bunting/ K. Wendy Popp
☐ *Our Eight Nights of Hanukkah* by Michael J. Rosen/ Dyanne Disalvo-Ryan
☐ *Papa's Latkes* by Michelle Edwards/ Stacey Schuett
☐ *Runaway Dreidel!* by Leslea Newman/ Kyrsten Brooker
☐ *The Trees of the Dancing Goats* by Patricia Polacco

Advent Week Four

The Nativity
☐ ✳ *The Christmas Bird* by Sallie Ketcham/ Stacey Schuett
☐ ✳ *Father and Son: A Nativity Story* by Geraldine McCaughrean/ Fabian Negrin
☐ ✳ *The Christmas Bird* by Bernadette Watts (OOP)
☐ ✳ **The Christmas Donkey by Gillian McClure (OOP)**
☐ ✳ **Mortimer's Christmas Manger by Karma Wilson/ Jan Chapman**
☐ **A Christmas Story by Brian Wildsmith**
☐ *All for the Newborn Baby* by Phyllis Root/ Nicola Bayley
☐ *Angela and the Baby Jesus* by Frank McCourt/ Raul Colon
☐ **Christmas Lullaby by Nancy Jewell/ Stefano Vitale (OOP)**
☐ **Draw Me a Star by Eric Carle**
☐ *Jacob's Gift* by Max Lucado/ Robert Hunt
☐ *Mary Did You Know* by Mark Lowry
☐ *Only a Star* by Margery Facklam/ Nancy Carpenter
☐ **Room for a Little One by Martin Waddell/ Jason Cockcroft**
☐ *Saint Francis and the Christmas Donkey* by Robert Byrd (Study guide found in *Catholic Mosaic*, available from www.hillsideeducation.com)
☐ *Saint Francis Celebrates Christmas* by Mary Caswell Walsh/ Helen Caswell
☐ *Silent Night* by Susan Jeffers
☐ *The Christmas Garland* by Lisa Flinn/ Barbara Younger
☐ *The Christmas Story* by Kay Chorao
☐ **The Crippled Lamb by Max Lucado/ Liz Bonahm** (Study guide found in *Catholic Mosaic*, available from www.hillsideeducation.com)
☐ **The Donkey's Dream by Barbara Helen Berger** (Study guide found in *Catholic Mosaic*, available from www.hillsideeducation.com)
☐ **The Friendly Beasts illustrated by Sharon McGinley**
☐ *The Huron Carol* illustrated by Frances Tyrrell
☐ *The Legend of the Christmas Rose* by William H. Hooks/ Richard Williams
☐ **The Little Donkey by Gerda Marie Scheidl/ Bernadette Watts**
☐ *The Tale of Three Trees* by Angela Elwell Hunt/ Tim Jonke (Study guide found in *Catholic Mosaic*, available from www.hillsideeducation.com)
☐ **The True Story of Christmas by Nell Navillus/ Allan Eitzen**
☐ *There Was No Snow on Christmas Eve* by Pam Munoz Ryan/ Dennis Nolan
☐ **To Hear the Angels Sing: A Christmas Poem by W. Nikola-Lisa/ Jill Weber**
☐ Tonight You Are My Baby: Mary's Christmas Gift by Jeannine Q. Norris/Tim Ladwig
☐ *Visions of Christmas* an art book published by Simon and Schuster
☐ *What Happened to Merry Christmas?* by Robert C. Baker/ Dave Hill

☐ *When It Snowed That Night* by Norma Farber/ Petra Mathers (a collection of Christmas poetry)
☐ *Who Was Born This Special Day?* by Eve Bunting

Angels
☐ ✳ **Bright Christmas: An Angel Remembers** by Andrew Clements/ Kate Kiesler
☐ **Angels, Angels Everywhere** by Tomie dePaola
☐ **Country Angel Christmas** by Tomie dePaola
☐ *The Littlest Angel* by Charles Tazewell/ Deborah Lanino
☐ **While Angels Watch** by Marni McGee/ Tina Macnaughton

Epiphany
☐ ✳ *Danny and the Kings* by Susan Cooper/ Jos. A. Smith (OOP)
☐ *Song of the Camels* by Elizabeth Coatsworth/ Anna Vojtech (OOP)
☐ *What Star Is This?* by Joseph Slate/ Alison Jay
☐ *The Last Straw* by Fredrick H. Thury/ Vlasta van Kampen (Study guide found in *Catholic Mosaic*, available from www.hillsideeducation.com)
☐ *The Visit of the Wise Men* by Martha Jander/ Lin Wang
☐ *Three Kings and a Star* by Fred Crump, Jr.
☐ *We Three Kings* by Gennady Spirin

Christmas Around the World

☐ ✳ *Waiting for Christmas* by Kathleen Long Bostrom/ Alexi Natchev (Germany)
☐ *A Kenya Christmas* by Tony Johnston/ Leonard Jenkins (Africa)
☐ *An Island Christmas* by Lynn Joseph/ Catherine Stock (Caribbean)
☐ *Baboushka: A Christmas Folktale from Russia* by Arthur Scholey/ Helen Cann (Russia)
☐ *Christmas in Noisy Village* by Astrid Lindgren/ Ilon Wikland (Sweden)
☐ *Lucia Morning in Sweden* by Ewa Rydaker (Sweden)
☐ *Marta and the Manger Straw: A Christmas Tradition from Poland* by Virginia Kroll/ Robyn Belton (Poland)
☐ *Miracle of the Poinsettia* by Brian Cavanaugh/ Dennis Rockhill (Mexico)
☐ *Nine Days to Christmas* by Marie Hall Ets/ Aurora Labastida (Mexico)
☐ *The Cajun Night before Christmas* by Trosclair/ James Rice (Louisiana)
☐ *The Christmas Drum: A Romanian Christmas Custom* by Maureen Brett Hooper/ Diane Paterson (OOP) (Romania)
☐ *The Huron Carol* illustrated by Frances Tyrrell (Huron Indian Tribe)
☐ *The Night of Las Posadas* by Tomie dePaola (Mexico)
☐ *The Santero's Miracle* by Rudolfo Anaya/ Amy Cordova (New Mexico)
☐ *Too Many Tamales* by Gary Soto/ Ed Martinez (South America)
☐ *What's Cooking, Jamela?* by Niki Daly (South Africa)

Older Children (Preteens and Teens) and Family Read Alouds

- [ ] ❄ *A Christmas Memory* by Truman Capote/ Beth Peck
- [ ] ❄ *The Trees Kneel at Christmas* by Maud Hart Lovelace
- [ ] ❄ *The Gift of the Magi* by O. Henry
- [ ] *A Christmas Carol* by Charles Dickens
- [ ] *A Little House Christmas* by Laura Ingalls Wilder/ Renee' Graft
- [ ] *A Little House Christmas Treasury* by Laura Ingalls Wilder
- [ ] *Bartholomew's Passage: A Family Story for Advent* by Arnold Ytreeide
- [ ] *Christmas Remembered* by Tomie dePaola
- [ ] *Cricket on the Hearth* by Charles Dickens
- [ ] *I Saw Three Ships* by Elizabeth Goudge (OOP)
- [ ] *Jan Brett's Christmas Treasury* by Jan Brett
- [ ] *Jotham's Journey: A Storybook for Advent* by Arnold Ytreeide
- [ ] *Letters from Father Christmas* by J. R. R. Tolkien
- [ ] *Maggie Rose, Her Birthday Christmas* by Ruth Sawyer
- [ ] *Papa's Angels* by Collin Wilcox Paxton/ Gary Carden
- [ ] *Sister Wendy's Story of Christmas,* found in *Adventures in Art* by Wendy Beckett
- [ ] *The Best Christmas Pageant Ever* by Barbara Robinson
- [ ] *The Christmas Doll* by Elvira Woodruff/ Barbara McClintock
- [ ] *The House Without a Christmas Tree* by Gail Rock/ Charles C. Gehm (OOP)
- [ ] *The Lion in the Box* by Marguerite De Angeli
- [ ] *The Silver Donkey* by Sonya Hartnett/ Don Powers
- [ ] *The Story of Holly and Ivy* by Rumer Godden
- [ ] *The Story of the Other Wise Man* by Henry van Dyke

Just For Fun

- [ ] **Bear Stays Up for Christmas by Karma Wilson/ Jane Chapman**
- [ ] *Santa and the Three Bears* by Dominic Catalano
- [ ] *The Jolly Christmas Postman* by Janet and Allan Ahlberg
- [ ] *The Legend of Papa Noel: A Cajun Christmas Story* by Terri Hoover Dunham/ Laura Knorr
- [ ] *The Mouse Before Christmas* by Michael Garland

Movies for Family Viewing

- [ ] Charles Dickens' *A Christmas Carol* (many versions available)
- [ ] *How the Grinch Stole Christmas* (Dr. Seuss' cartoon version)
- [ ] *It's a Wonderful Life*
- [ ] *Miracle on 34th Street*
- [ ] *The Christmas Story*
- [ ] *The House without a Christmas Tree*
- [ ] *The Little Drummer Boy*
- [ ] *The Polar Express*
- [ ] *The Walton's Homecoming*

Various Versions of "Twas the Night Before Christmas"

☐ *The Cajun Night before Christmas* by Trosclair/ James Rice
☐ *The New Cajun Night before Christmas* by E.A. Giroux/ Ernie Eldredge
☐ *The Night Before Christmas* by James Marshall
☐ *The Night Before Christmas* illustrated by Jan Brett
☐ *The Night Before Christmas* illustrated by Tasha Tudor

Jan Brett Christmas Books

Christmas Trolls
Gingerbread Baby
Jan Brett's Christmas Treasury
Noelle of the Nutcracker
The Mitten
The Night before Christmas
The Three Snow Bears
The Twelve Days of Christmas
The Wild Christmas Reindeers
Who's that Knocking on Christmas Eve?

For an enjoyable treat, take some time this Christmas season to peruse Jan Brett's website with your children (http://www.janbrett.com/) where you will find many free printable coloring and craft sheets and a lot of inspiration.

Tomie dePaola Christmas Books

Angels, Angels Everywhere
Christmas Remembered
Country Angel Christmas
Get Dressed, Santa!
Hark! A Christmas Sampler
Jingle the Christmas Clown
Merry Christmas, Strega Nona
Pages of Music
The Clown of God
The First Christmas
The Friendly Beast
The Legend of Old Befana
The Legend of the Poinsettia
The Night of Las Posadas
The Story of the Three Wise Kings
Tomie's Little Christmas Pageant
Tony's Bread

Arlington Catholic Herald columnist, Elizabeth Foss, has written a Tomie de Paola Advent /Epiphany Literature Unit Study available at http://charlottemason.tripod.com/4realpaola.htm. This unit will take you and your child through a wonderland of Advent/Christmas/Epiphany reading, crafting, baking, and sharing and leave you with many joyful memories.

~ Notes ~

~ Your Personal Booklist ~

- [ ] _____
- [ ] _____
- [ ] _____
- [ ] _____
- [ ] _____
- [ ] _____
- [ ] _____
- [ ] _____
- [ ] _____
- [ ] _____
- [ ] _____
- [ ] _____
- [ ] _____
- [ ] _____
- [ ] _____
- [ ] _____
- [ ] _____
- [ ] _____
- [ ] _____
- [ ] _____
- [ ] _____

- [ ] _____
- [ ] _____
- [ ] _____
- [ ] _____
- [ ] _____
- [ ] _____
- [ ] _____
- [ ] _____
- [ ] _____
- [ ] _____
- [ ] _____
- [ ] _____
- [ ] _____
- [ ] _____
- [ ] _____
- [ ] _____
- [ ] _____
- [ ] _____
- [ ] _____
- [ ] _____
- [ ] _____
- [ ] _____

 Selected Annotations

~ Month of December ~

Christmas in the Stable
Selected and Illustrated by Beverly K. Duncan
This collection of dearly loved Christmas poetry, this book should be on everyone's shelf. The pages of poetry are surrounded by borders that have been inspired by medieval manuscripts. Duncan weaves the legends and tales of various flowers into the borders "As they have long stood for the birth of the One who is forever." Don't miss the explanation at the book's end. This book should be read along with *When It Snowed That Night* and *All for the Newborn Baby.*

~ Advent Week One ~

~ Decoration and Preparation Stories ~

✸ *Cobweb Christmas: The Tradition of Tinsel*
Written by Shirley Como/ Illustrated by Jane Manning
This is a quaint German fairytale that relates the legend of why we place tinsel on the Christmas tree. Tante lives in a cottage on the edge of a forest and cannot even count all the Christmases she has seen. That is the one time every year she does a clean sweep of her cottage and prepares for Christmas. "Time to make Christmas. Time to share Christmas. Time to wait for Christmas." This is her motto. But one Christmas, Tante wants some Christmas magic that is "not of her own making." When the rooster wakes Tante on Christmas morn, she sees the beautiful magical tinsel that Christkindel and the Christmas spiders have left for her. Now each year she nods her head when it is "Time for Christmas magic." This out-of-print book should be read with *The Christmas Cobwebs* by Odds Bodkin.

✸ *The Christmas Cobwebs*
Written by Odds Bodkin/ Illustrated by Terry Widener
When a fire destroys a cobbler's home, he and his family end up on the street at Christmas time. The one thing the cobbler rescues from the flames is a precious wooden box of Christmas ornaments brought to America from the old country. With no home and no money, the cobbler is forced to sell the contents of the box in order to feed his family. That Christmas, his family has only a bare tree in a corner of the old building in which they stay. But there is a Christmas surprise hanging from the rafters that will delight your children's imagination. This book should be read with *Cobweb Christmas* by Shirley Como.

✴ *The Cobweb Curtain*
Written by Jenny Koralek/ Illustrated by Pauline Baynes

There is talk in town that a new king has been born and King Herod begins a deadly search party in an effort to locate him. A young shepherd knows this is a matter of life and death to the newborn baby he saw in the stable, so he leads the family to a nearby cave where they hide from the authorities. A humble spider sees and hears all outside the cave and spins a cobweb curtain over the door to provide for the baby's warmth. During the cold night the nighttime dew settles and freezes on the web and makes an icy curtain which fools the soldiers into believing it has been there for some time. Read this book to see how the shepherd saves the Holy Family and brings the cobweb curtain home to his own family. An enchanting story.

Christmas Tree Memories
Written and Illustrated by Aliki

What can I say about this book? I love it. It's everything I love about the season and the joy of decorating for the holidays. Each ornament upon the Christmas tree brings back memories to the family who sits around it. The illustrations are stunning and rich. It is a delightful book to be read with your children on the sofa after you have decorated your own Christmas tree.

Christmas Is . . .
Written and Illustrated by Gail Gibbons

You can't go wrong with a book by Gail Gibbons. The first page hits the mark with: "Christmas is . . . The Christ Child" and the story of the nativity. From there, Gibbons covers a wide variety of Christmas ideas and symbols. This would be a good companion read for the younger set, while *The Twenty-Four Days before Christmas* by Madeleine L'Engle/ Joe DeVelasco is offered for older readers.

Christmas Tree Farm
Written by Ann Purmell/ Illustrated by Jill Weber

Is the annual Christmas Tree Farm outing a tradition at your house? If so, this book is a must-read before you leave on your expedition. This book explains how Christmas trees are grown and tended all year long then harvested at Christmas time. At the back of the book is a section on "Christmas Tree Lore," "Christmas Tree Facts," and "Christmas Tree Time Line." Not only fun to read, it will teach you more about Christmas trees than you thought there was to know. Makes me want to have an "old-time tree-trimming party" at my house! This books goes well with a reading of *Night Tree* by Eve Bunting.

Deck the Halls:An Old Welsh Carol illustrated by Iris Van Rynbach
The illustrations in this book are cheery and inviting and detailed enough to calm the most energetic child. Play the carol as background music while enjoying this book together. Perfect for preschoolers.

Mother Hubbard's Christmas
Written and Illustrated by John O'Brien
I thought this book was too cute not to mention. It's a delightful sing-song with Christmas rhymes replacing the traditional Old Mother Hubbard nursery rhyme. Young children will appreciate Mother Hubbard's frantic Christmas preparations and relate to her dog's childlike behavior. Provides a chance to compare and contrast this Christmas version to the traditional 14-stanza rhyme.

Waiting for Noel: An Advent Story
Written by Ann Dixon/ Illustrated by Mark Graham
This story encompasses the waiting, anticipation, and preparation that Advent brings as well as the waiting, anticipation, and preparation that come with a new baby. While lighting the Advent candles, Noel's father shares the story of how her family awaited her birth. A great read for children born in December.

Apple Tree Christmas
Written and Illustrated by Trinka Hakes Noble
This book is a delight to the spirit as well as the eyes. Noble's artwork stands out with the whimsical warmth and charm a reader expects to find in a Christmas book. When a family loses their apple tree in a storm, the father drops his other work to salvage the fruits of the tree. This book has rich artwork, poignant family closeness, and a nostalgic storyline. The reader will find the sweetness of this Christmas story satisfying to the very end.

The Little Christmas Tree
Written by Karl Ruhmann/ Illustrated by Anne Moller
This is the perfect Christmas book for children to grow up with. A small child on the edge of a big world can relate to being the smallest tree on the edge of a big forest. This book is a great companion read for Shel Silverstein's *The Giving Tree* and Eve Bunting's *Night Tree.*

The Fir Tree
Written by Hans Christian Andersen/ Adapted and Illustrated by Bernadette Watts
The little fir tree in the forest is reminded by those trees greater than it to rejoice and be happy with his young life. But the little fir tree can only think of growing tall and splendid. It is finally tall and wonderful and selected to be a family's Christmas tree after which it is discarded in the attic and then outdoors. The tree begins to realize how good life was in the forest. It misses its former life and, as the fire consumes the former Christmas tree, "…the branches sighed and cracked as if the heart of the tree were breaking." This little tale will help to encourage children to be happy in the present and not to fret too anxiously over the future. Written by Hans Christian Andersen, this classic tale has many adaptations you will want to be on the lookout for. I encourage families to select their favorite version by finding an adaptation faithful to Andersen's then carefully observing the illustrations.

The Attic Christmas
Written by B. G. Hennessy/ Illustrated by Dan Andreasen
Children often fancy the idea of toys and objects coming to life. This little book related the story of a collection of Christmas ornaments that have found themselves tucked away in the attic, having to celebrate Christmas after Christmas without a family. They remember fondly the sights and smells of many happy Christmases long ago and, as they wait for someone to find them, they remember a babe without a home and a bed. Will someone find them and welcome them back into the fold? Read this storybook to find out.

The Year of the Perfect Christmas Tree
Written by Gloria Houston/ Illustrated by Barbara Cooney
This beautifully told Appalachian tale introduce us to Ruthie and her Papa as they go into the woods to pick out a tree for the church's Christmas. Then as the story continues, Papa must go off to the Great War. When he does not arrive home before Christmas, Ruthie and her Mama must go to cut the tree down and haul it to the church. Will a present be upon the tree for Ruthie? And will Papa get home in time to see Ruthie play the heavenly angel in the Christmas play? This book is a family favorite.

One Splendid Tree
Written by Marilyn Helmer/ Illustrated by Dianne Eastman
This is another war-time Christmas story. Father is away at war and the family is struggling financially—a new experience for them. With money too scarce to even get a Christmas tree, Hattie and Junior, the brother and sister in the story, decide to dress up an a "droopy old plant into a Christmas tree" and leave it in the hallway so that everyone living in the tiny apartment building can enjoy it. The simple act makes Hattie feel much better about her new living conditions and brings cheer to the air. The occupants of the building begin to contribute decorations of their own to the "droopy old plant," turning it into a thing of beauty and good cheer. Eastman's wonderful photo-collage artwork is a perfect fit with this wonderful story and there are directions found in the back so you can make your own snowman, just like Momma does in the story.

Christmas Tapestry
Written and Illustrated by Patricia Polacco
This book is another excellent Christmas addition to your Christmas reading list. As in *An Orange for Frankie* and many of her other books, Polacco retells a story handed down through generations. Jonathan Jefferson Weeks can't possibly imagine why they had to leave their home in Memphis to come to Detroit. His father believes that there is a purpose in all things under God's plan. Jonathan can't imagine what that purpose is, especially after a blizzard ruins the church wall right before the Christmas Eve services. When Jonathan and his father find a hand-stitched embroidery cloth in an antique shop that would perfectly cover the damaged stain and hole on the church wall, Jonathan is given a hint of the blessings yet to come on this night of miracles. Enter two survivors of the Holocaust and discover how this Christmas tapestry wraps its symbolism and miracle around both the Weeks family and a Jewish family on this holiest night of the year. It's a tale every family will remember long after the book is back on the shelf.

The Legend of the Poinsettia
Written and Illustrated by Tomie dePaola
In this beautiful holiday story, Lucida is proud that her mother has been asked to help make a new blanket for baby Jesus in the *la Navidad* Christmas play. Her joy is short-lived when her mother becomes sick and cannot finish the blanket. Lucida tries to finish it but her attempts meet with failure. Heartbroken, she must go to the *la Navidad* play with nothing but a patch of tall green weeds—her only offering to the baby Jesus. The weeds are miraculously transformed, however, and the poinsettia blooms.

The Little Match Girl
Written by Hans Christian Andersen/ Illustrated by Rachel Isadora
The Little Match Girl is one of my fondest childhood reads. In the story, an innocent child longs for comfort, warmth, love, and beauty but is exposed, instead, to harsh conditions, bitter cold, absence of love, and ugliness. The comfort of home, the warmth of the stove and roasted goose, the beauty of a Christmas tree, and the loving arms of a grandmother will touch every heart that lives in this imperfect world yet longs for the ideal vision of comfort, warmth, love, and beauty that only heaven and God can give.

Christmas in the Country
Written by Cynthia Rylant/ Illustrated by Diane Goode
"Winter in the country is so quiet" and so is the message in this book. The lovely pictures by Goode are wrapped in a snowy haze, thus accenting the family blissful preparations for Christmas. A nice, quiet book to cuddle with on a cold winter night.

Advent Week Two

~ Giving ~

✳ The Shoemaker's Dream
Adapted by Mildred Schell/ Illustrated by Masahiro Kasuya
This is an old classic that many parents will remember. Martin, the town's shoemaker, has a dream. Jesus appears to him and tells him that He will visit Martin the next day. Martin is excited and eager to welcome Jesus into his humble home. While he waits and works, he is visited by an old man, a mother and her baby, and a woman and boy. Martin welcomes them into his home and gives them food, drink, warmth, and counsel. At night he goes to bed, disappointed that Jesus never came. But Jesus appears to him once again in his dream and thanks Martin for feeding Him, giving Him warm clothing and shelter, and for addressing His needs. This dear story is an effective way to teach children the Scripture passage found in Matthew 25:40: And the King will answer them, 'Truly I say to you, as you did it to one of the least of these my brethren, you did it to me.'

✴ *A Small Miracle*
Written by Peter Collington
This wordless picture book is perfect for fostering Christmas meditation. In a magical tale, a poor gypsy woman's hard life is made a little easier on Christmas night through the help of unlikely beings. This story is about teaching the Golden Rule to your children: "Do unto others as you would have them do to you."

✴ *The Christmas Candle*
Written by Richard Paul Evans/ Illustrated by Jacob Collins
In this book, Thomas is in a hurry to get home. He has little time and no patience for beggars and the poor. Needing a light to find his way, Thomas stops in a candle shop, He scoffs at the fancy Christmas candles that "devour themselves." The chandler (the candle maker) offers him a cheaper candle but warns him that he "may find it costly." On his way home, Thomas begins to realize there is something strange about the candle he carries. His path home teaches him and the reader that we are indeed "our brother's keeper."

✴ *Why the Chimes Rang*
Written by Raymond MacDonald Alden
The village people have all heard the tales of the bells ringing at Christmas time when someone places the "greatest and best offering" on the altar. But is it only a legend? No one has heard the chimes ring in ages. Then one year two brothers get the opportunity to go to the old church for the Christmas festivities but, on the way, they come upon an old lady who has fallen in the snow and needs help. What will they do? They are torn between missing the festivities and helping the old lady. This story rings, as do the bells, with the real meaning of Christmas giving. A classic that has been brought back to life, this book will delight your family.

✴ *The First Christmas Stocking*
Written by Elizabeth Winthrop/ Bagram Ibatoulline
This story is one of my favorites. Claire's family is very poor, but, as Claire's mother teaches her daughter to knit and "Dream your dreams," she teaches her little girl to knit her dreams straight into the wool of each stocking she makes. After Claire's mother dies, knitting proves to be the only connection Claire has with her mother. When Claire makes a loving gift of her work, many others are blessed by her dreams. Claire realizes finally that her mother is knit into her and never far away.

✴ *The Bear's Christmas Surprise*
Written by Bruno Hachler/ Illustrated by Angela Kehlenbeck
On Christmas Eve night, while people sleep, some old stuffed teddy bears climb off their shelves and out of their toy boxes and go out into the night on a mission. What they do might surprise young readers! But, by story's end, the warmth and love that this story evokes will prompt most people heart to look beyond their homes on Christmas day. The message in this story is reminiscent of that of *The Velveteen Rabbit*.

✹ *The Christmas Coat* (OOP)
Written by Clyde Robert Bulla/ Illustrated by Sylvie Wickstrom
Mama works so hard and all she wants is for her boys to behave themselves and get along. But the boys try her patience until, in a fight over a Christmas coat; they make a terrible mistake. When they work together to fix it, they learn a valuable lesson.

Jingle the Christmas Clown
Written and Illustrated by Tomie dePaola
Poor little Jingle is too small to perform in the circus. His job is to care for the circus animal babies. On Christmas Eve, Jingle and the baby animals are left in a deserted town to rest while the other circus members travel to perform in the nearby city. Jingle's heart goes out to the few elderly townspeople who will not have a Christmas celebration in their town this year. He puts together a free Christmas performance for the townspeople, complete with a living Christmas tree. This book is Tomie dePaola at his best!

The Little Drummer Boy
Illustrated by Ezra Jack Keats
You know the song—now put pictures to the words. I especially like Keats' depiction of Mary as she nods her consent to the little drummer boy. Complete with a musical accompaniment at the end, this pictorial song remind us that in each one of us is a special gift fit to give the newborn King.

December
Written by Eve Bunting/ Illustrated by David Diaz
A story of a mother and her son, this book brings your child out of your cozy home and into a cardboard box where a homeless family lives. All their little makeshift box affords them is a plate with two Christmas cookies on it and a poor branch for a Christmas tree. On Christmas Eve, they share the hospitality of their cardboard box and their two Christmas cookies with an elderly homeless woman. In the morning, the old woman is gone, but the luminous presence of a familiar singing angel is in the opening to the box. If you like books about Christmas angels, you will love this book.

Hannah's Bookmobile Christmas
Written by Sally Derby/ Illustrated by Gabi Swiatkowska
The bookmobile rolls along the roads where the snowflakes float "like dandelion" as people wait to collect their books before the storm hits town. Each of the bookmobile visitors has a little gift to offer Mary, the bookmobile operator, and her eight-year-old niece Hannah. On the way home, they find themselves stuck in the snow and facing a long night in the bookmobile. That's when they realize that with the gifts their customers gave them, they have food to keep them until morning. And they are surrounded by books. What better way to spend a wintry night!

The Gingerbread Doll
Written by Susan Tews/ Illustrated by Megan Lloyd
Little Rebecca has dreams of getting a porcelain doll under the Christmas tree, but times are hard and money is scarce. Instead she receives a gingerbread doll whom she grows to love. After all, gingerbread must be treated as tenderly as porcelain. But the doll finally

does get broken and Rebecca carefully puts away the scrap cloth dress with the mismatched buttons. Even after Rebecca finally gets the beautiful porcelain doll, she always remembers her "best doll", gingerbread Button Marie. This book is for every little girl who loves a doll.

A Christmas Gift for Mama
Written by Lauren Thompson/ Illustrated by Jim Burke
This is a rather lengthy storybook which echoes *The Gift of the Magi* by O. Henry. In place of the wife is a child. In place of the husband is a mother. In place of the beautiful hair is a beloved doll. In place of the watch is a beloved china lady. The mother and daughter sacrifice what they love the most to make Christmas happy for the other. As the author notes at the end of the story: "It is an ode to the ultimate value not of presents but of presence, not of gifts but of the heart that gives all."

The Clown of God
Written and Illustrated by Tomie dePaola
In this poignant story, poor Giovanni represents each one of us. We really have nothing to offer Christ but our talents and our love. Like Giovanni, sometimes our cares in the world make us lose sight of our real purpose in life. Giovanni teaches us that we should seek to make those around us happy because, by doing so, we make Christ happy—and Christ is the ultimate audience.

Pages of Music
Written by Tony Johnston/ Illustrated by Tomie dePaola
Paolo and his mother celebrate art and life on the island of Sardinia where the humble shepherds in the field share their bread and (fogli di musica) *pages of music* while Paolo leads a joyful life on his beloved island. He grows up to become a famous musician but does not forget the bread and music the shepherds shared with him and his mother. Neither does he forget his promise: "One day I will go back there." So one Christmas day he returns and shares his *fogli di musica* with his friends, the shepherds.

Stephen's Feast
Written by Jean Richardson/ Illustrated by Alice Englander
Young Stephen is looking forward to the merry-making in the palace on the Feast of St. Stephen. But his plans change when Good King Wenceslas takes young Stephen into his confidence to ask him to help a poor beggar the night of the celebrations. Stephen realizes the joy of giving and discovers that the feast in the peasant's cottage is more magical than the feast in the palace's Big Hall.

A Child's Christmas at St. Nicholas Circle
Written by Douglas Kaine McKelvey/ Paintings by Thomas Kinkade
This is a nostalgic trip back to 1918. Brought to life by old-fashioned photographs of the characters and set against the backdrop of the paintings of Thomas Kinkade, this story is about a little boy whose thoughts and wishes are centered on himself on this holiday season. Until he encounters a lost child who shows him that Christmas is much more than this. Its message of sharing and caring will not be lost on young children.

~ Santa Claus ~

✶ *Santa's Favorite Story*
Written by Hisako Aoki/ Illustrated by Ivan Gantschev
The forest animals are excited about another Christmas filled with presents, but Santa Claus knows that Christmas is about so much more. He is anxious that his friends in the forest learn the true meaning of Christmas and that it is—that it is "better than any presents I can ever deliver." A keeper.

Santa and the Three Bears
Written and Illustrated by Dominic Catalano
This is a new twist to an old tale. Three bears, lumbering along, wonder into a house decked with a festive table of goodies and a workshop full of toys, crafts, and paint. Find out what the jolly man and his wife do when they discover these three unexpected guests in their home on Christmas Eve.

~ St. Nicholas ~

The Miracle of Saint Nicholas
Written by Gloria Whelan/ Illustrated by Judith Brown
Although her village church stands deserted in Soviet Russia, Alexi's babushka has dreams of it becoming once again the church from her childhood: lit with candles and full of family and friends. Alexi sets out to make his babushka's "miracle" happen. His work to restore the church motivates the other villagers to reveal secrets that they have kept hidden for many, many years. And the shoemaker has the biggest secret of all. This story is a delightful read.

~ Advent Week Three ~

~ Family ~

✶ *An Orange for Frankie*
Written and Illustrated by Patricia Polacco
As soon as I read this book, I knew it had to be a featured *Mosaic* title. Many children want to know if a story is true. This story is. And its message is eternal, a story of family love and forgiveness. Don't miss the author's note at the front and back of book. The pictures are traditional Polacco: bright, colorful, and full of life.

✶ *Silent Night*
Written and Illustrated by Will Moses
Mama is about to give birth to a Christmas baby and the whole town is aflutter with anticipation. Grandma and the doctor arrive in time for the birth and the new baby arrives

in time for Christmas. As the family gives gifts to the newborn baby, Andy realizes he does not have anything for his new baby sister. Then, again, perhaps he can give her something better; the promise and gift of himself.

✴ *The Twenty-Four Days before Christmas*
Written by Madeleine L'Engle/ Illustrated by Joe DeVelasco
The Austin household is dancing with Christmas plans and Vicky is going to be a Christmas angel in the school play, and the whole family is awaiting the birth of a very special Christmas baby. But what happens if the baby keeps Momma from the school play and from spending Christmas with the family. This book is a cozy read for the whole family.

✴ *The Christmas Promise*
Written by Susan Bartoletti/ Illustrated by David Christiana
During the Great Depression, a father is down on his luck, with no job, no money, and a young daughter to care for. And so they hop on boxcars and travel from town to town in search of something good. Poppa teaches his daughter what the chalked hobo signs mean (these signs can be found inside the book's cover). And his daughter wonders: "Do hoboes have Christmas?" Her father promises he will find a way for his little hobo daughter to have a Christmas and, in doing so, he teaches her never to give up hoping for a better tomorrow.

✴ *One Christmas Dawn*
Written by Candice Ransom/ Illustrated by Peter Fiore
This book tells a Christmas story about a family that learns that Christmas is all about being together. Sadly, this book is out-of-print but if you come across a copy at your library or at a book sale, snatch it up. The imagery in this book is superb. This book is wonderful at helping young minds to see how an author "shows" the story to the reader versus "telling" the story.

✴ *Night Tree*
Written by Eve Bunting/ Illustrated by Ted Rand
Eve Bunting truly captures the essence of childhood in her books: family, simple pleasures, and the wonder of God's creation. This book made me long to find a tree in the forest for our family to share the blessings and riches of Christmas with all of God's creatures. Children will love this story.

The Christmas Box
Written and Illustrated by JoAnne Stewart Wetzel
The Christmas Box is a story waiting to be opened and enjoyed. This book is based on a true story and does not disappoint our expectations. The children in the story anxiously await Christmas morning when they can open a gift from their father. The children's father is a soldier stationed in Japan so the line "Inside was Japan" tells us immediately what's inside the box. The Christmas box holds much more than items from Japan—it brings Daddy home in a physical sense, if only for one day. This is a great book for military families whose loved ones are away from home during the holidays.

My Prairie Christmas
Written by Brett Harvey/ Illustrated by Deborah Kogan Ray

This is the story of a little girl's first Christmas out on the endless prairie. It's so very different from the Christmases she remembers back in Maine that she is worried about many things, most of all, where will they get a Christmas tree on that "ocean of grass." There are no cranberries on the prairie for stringing and their "box of shiny ornaments" is way back in Maine. But Mama has lots of good ideas and she keeps the children busy while Papa goes off to find a Christmas tree. While they stay busy and wait, a blizzard comes shrieking across the prairie. Will Papa find his way safely home? All of a sudden, Elenore realizes that being together as a family is more important than having a Christmas tree. All ends well in this beautiful little Christmas story. Lovers of the Little House books will treasure this story. A must read.

The Log Cabin Christmas
Written by Ellen Howard

This book portrays a home without a mother: Mam has died. The family is sullen, but Elvirey is determined to embrace Christmas just as Mam had done when she was alive by doing doing the simple things she is able to do: light a candle and spread warmth back into the home. What is a home without the joy, love, and beauty of Christmas? This book shows us why we "need" Christmas. This book is a witness to what one person can do to spread Christmas cheer even when the night looks bleak and lonely.

An Ellis Island Christmas
Written by Maxinne Rhea Leighton/ Illustrated by Dennis Nolan

This book is more about a Polish family coming to American than about Christmas. The publisher recommends it for children ages 3-8, but it's a great read for older children as well. It is an excellent book showing a family's path to America and the gift of family at Christmas time.

~ Hanukkah ~

✶ *Toby Belfer Never had a Christmas Tree*
Written by Gloria Teles Pushker/ Illustrated by Judith Hierstein

The whole neighborhood is preparing for Christmas, but Toby Belfer feels left out. Her family does not observe Christmas because they are Jewish—so Toby Belfer has never had a Christmas tree. Her grandmother comes to the rescue, though. This book invites you and your child to come to Toby's Hanukkah party and learn about the very same holiday that Jesus and His family celebrated. Directions for making potato latkas, playing the traditional game of dreidel, and building a big menorah candleholder are included in the book.

Hanukkah Lights, Hanukkah Nights
Written by Leslie Kimmelman/ Illustrated by John Himmelman
This book is short and sweet but perfect for wiggly toddlers who want "one more" story before bedtime. Using a day-by-day format that preschoolers love, it offers a simple explanation of a family observing Hanukkah.

~ Advent Week Four ~

~ The Nativity ~

✱ *The Christmas Bird*
Written by Sallie Ketcham/Illustrated by Stacey Schuett
A little bird is lost on his flight south and a stable offers shelter. On this cold, dark night, he finds a newborn baby and his parents. He is moved to fan the flames of the campfire to warm the newborn baby and is rewarded for his kindness.

✱ *Father and Son*
Written by Geraldine McCaughrean/ Illustrated by Fabian Negrin
How many renditions of the nativity focus on Mary and Jesus? In this newer version, the author takes a look at the relationship between Joseph and Jesus. What does a father teach us? What role do the father's hands have in the upbringing of his child? A different take on a familiar story, this book is a refreshing and meaningful read.

✱ *The Christmas Bird*
Written and Illustrated by Bernadette Watts
This book follows a little girl to a stable with a gift for the newborn King but, before she arrives, her gift is broken. In return for her kindness and thoughtfulness, the newborn King rewards her with His own gifts of song and joy.

✱ *The Christmas Donkey*
Written and Illustrated by Gillian McClure
Here's another sweet donkey story that shouldn't be overlooked, even though it's out-of-print. Arod is your typical "wild and proud" child—only he's a donkey. Arod's bragging and boasting annoys those around him. He must go through a humbling process before he can realize that God's in control. In the end, Arod realizes it is through God's glory and not his own that he is privileged and blessed. Children can learn an important message from this little book.

✱ *Mortimer's Christmas Manger*
Written by Karma Wilson/ Illustrated by Jan Chapman
Think of everything you've ever loved about Christmas—this little book has it all. Mortimer is a sweet little mouse looking for a "house just my size!" He climbs the Christmas tree to reach the stable housing the nativity. When he finds just some old

statues taking up space, he removes the baby from the manger in order to have a bed to sleep on. After hearing the father read the Christmas story, Mortimer gives the bed back to the Christ Child and scurries off, praying for another "house just my size," only to find a gingerbread house. This book is a sweet treat for December. Preschoolers will love it!

To Hear the Angels Sing: A Christmas Poem
Written by W. Nikola-Lisa/ Illustrated by Jill Weber
This is a simple poem that follows the timeline of the nativity story. The pictures are beautiful and colorful.

The Friendly Beasts
Illustrated by Sharon McGinley
There are many illustrated versions of this ancient Christmas carol, including one by Tomie dePaola. Each animal offers the Christ Child something that only that animal can give. I found this book illustrated by Sharon McGinley to be bright and colorful. It treats the ancient Christmas carol with beauty and grace. The use of repetition and the gifts of the animals will endear this book to your child. Parents are encouraged to read the author's note found in the back.

The Donkey's Dream
Written and Illustrated by Barbara Helen Berger
Using simple yet beautifully profound prose, the author gives careful consideration to the various Marian symbols from the Litany of Mary. A donkey dreams of each of the symbols as he carries Mary to Bethlehem. The author has included clues to the *les yeux de Marie* (Mary's eyes) which are sprinkled throughout the book. Its message is a wonderful one to hear in honor of the Mother of our Lord.

The Crippled Lamb
Written by Max Lucado/ Illustrated by Liz Bonahm
Who can deny the appeal of a lamb, especially a crippled lamb, who befriends a wise old cow named Abigail. When Josh, the crippled lamb, is unable to follow the other farm animals on to greener pastures, he is forced to stay behind with Abigail and sleep in the barn. But what a wondrous night to sleep in the old barn—the same wondrous night when a couple finds shelter in the old barn and Josh finds his rightful place beside a newborn babe. You and your children will enjoy this sweet nativity story.

The Christmas Story
Adapted and Illustrated by Kay Chorao
I am very picky about my nativity stories. I like the story to follow the proper sequence of events. I want the Christmas story to begin with the Annunciation and end with the family safely back in their homeland. I don't like Joseph to appear too old. I want the angels to be beautiful. I want Mary to be beautiful (and preferably with a blue mantle). I want Herod and all his villains to be in the story so children can see God's providence in action. Now your requirements for the perfect nativity story may differ from mine, but I think we can safely agree that we all like our Christmas story to follow Sacred Scripture.

This book fits all my requirements perfectly. Even if your requirements are a little different, I'm sure you will find this a pleasing adaptation of the blessed nativity.

The Christmas Garland
Written by Lisa Flinn/ Illustrated by Barbara Younger
While braiding garlands as her mother taught her, Hannah witnesses angels in the sky announcing the birth of a baby. With her father, Hannah visits the babe and leaves a garland with the baby's mother. There is no further storyline to this book—it is simply another retelling of the nativity. Still, it is a sweet story if you come across it.

The Huron Carol
Illustrated by Frances Tyrrell
This beautifully illustrated book brings life to the unique Christmas carol written by Jesuit missionary, Fr. Jean de Brebuef. This priest lived and worked with the Huron Indians and, in teaching them the Christian faith, brought the story of Christmas in the context of Huron beliefs so that the Indians could embrace Christ as their own Lord and Savior. The Huron Carol was sung by tribes long after Fr. Brebeuf's death and is still remembered and sung today. A simple piano accompaniment can be found in the back of the book.

All for the Newborn Baby
Written by Phyllis Root/ Illustrated by Nicola Bayley
This is a nature lover's nativity book. The author remembers the miracle of Jesus' birth and explores many carols and stories from various countries. From them she creates a lovely lullaby of folklore and nature symbols "all for the newborn baby." Beautiful.

There Was No Snow on Christmas Eve
Written by Pam Munoz Ryan/ Illustrated by Dennis Nolan
Most of us associate Christmas with snow. Snow has a magical effect. It's beautiful and pure like Jesus himself. But this book reminds us that "there was no snow on Christmas Eve." Ryan's magical language blended with Nolan's illuminating art takes us to "a night serene" and "a stable open to the world." This book is simple but its simplicity makes children aware that the nature of Christmas is not found in the weather but in the "awaited birth."

Visions of Christmas: Renaissance Triptychs
Published by Simon and Schuster
This book features the annunciation, visitation, nativity, adoration, epiphany, and the flight to Egypt. Using a lift-the-flap format, each event is rendered in beautiful Renaissance artwork, taking your child through the whole Christmas story from start to finish.

When it Snowed that Night
Written by Norma Farber/ Illustrated by Petra Mathers
This lovely book is a collection of poetry about the animals and wild life that bounds to the manger scene to worship the newborn King. Your child will be entertained as he

follows the stork, the ladybug, camel, sloth, turtle, giraffe, dove, spider, cricket, lamb, and hog to the manger and observes how they served the newborn King. For mothers who read this book, they will find a beautiful "ode to motherhood" just for them because there is one person who does not venture into the snow that night to travel to Bethlehem but God blesses her just the same. Beautiful and poetic.

Saint Francis and the Christmas Donkey
Written and Illustrated by Robert Byrd
This lovely find for any family captures the same pleasure children find in stories and pictures of Noah's Ark: There are animals galore. The donkey in this story is a sad creature who has caused his own tale of woe but, by story's end, he has made amends for his prideful and vain behavior and been redeemed by Christ. Do not overlook the Author's Note at the end, even if your children don't want to sit and listen. You will find a lot of interesting information there about the story and St. Francis.

Silent Night
Illustrated by Susan Jeffers
In mute, slate blue tones, Jeffers gives you and your child a rich visual to enjoy while listening to this timeless hymn.

~ Epiphany ~

✴ *Danny and the Kings*
Written by Susan Cooper/ Illustrated by Jos. A. Smith
This is a wonderful book for boys, especially those with brothers. Danny wants his little brother to have a Christmas tree but the family is too poor. Through the kindness of three "Kings of the Road" (simple truckers) journeying East, the family is blessed with a Christmas tree and the gift of the magi. A heartwarming story for the whole family.

The Last Straw
Written by Fredrick H. Thury/ Illustrated by Vlasta van Kampen
Dear old Hoshmakaka is a weary old camel plagued by aching joints, gout, and a dreadful sciatica nerve problem. He is happy to sleep most of the time, compete in water-drinking contests, and attend the local cud-chewing convention. What a relaxed life he leads! Until voices in the desert sand tell him that he has been chosen to "carry gifts to a baby king." And dear old Hoshmakaka grudgingly answers their call. Every hour on the hour someone blocks his path and asks him to take his/her gift to the newborn king. Complaining of his joints, his gout, his sciatica every step of the way; he slowly makes his way across the desert. It's a Christmas story you simply have to read.

~ Angels ~

✱ *Bright Christmas: An Angel Remembers*
Written by Andrew Clements/ Illustrated by Kate Kiesler
In a beautiful adaptation of the Christmas story, an angel remembers that first Christmas night. The angel reminds us that where angels live "there's really no time at all. It is just now . . . it is still that first Christmas night." Beautiful and soothing. Makes a great lullaby story.

Angels, Angels Everywhere
Written and Illustrated by Tomie dePaola
Every preschooler in your house will love this colorful book. The varieties of angels (music, kitchen, garden, tea party, bath) that do chores of love around the house fly about the pages with artistic grace and flair.

Country Angel Christmas
Written and Illustrated by Tomie dePaola
St. Nicholas tells the youngest angels that they are responsible for the Christmas celebration in Heaven. Feeling they are not important enough for such a big undertaking, the little angels are worried. What can they possibly do to compete with the past Christmas celebrations? The angels set to work—but the three smallest angels are repeatedly told to "stay out of the way." In the end, St. Nicholas makes sure these three littlest angels have the most important job of all.

The Littlest Angel
Written by Charles Tazewell/ Illustrated by Deborah Lanino (several other illustrated versions of this story are available)
Time magazine called this story an "international classic." This book follows a little angel who is testing his wings in heaven and fumbling miserably along. When the Christ Child is born, the angels hurry to prepare their gifts to present before the throne of God. The littlest angel's gift is but a simple wooden box that carries the things he held dear in his earthly life: a butterfly, a blue egg, two white stones, and the collar of his faithful dog. But this humble little gift has the power to dazzle the heavens and everything below it.

~ Christmas Around the World ~

✱ *Waiting for Christmas*
Written by Kathleen Long Bostrom/Illustrated by Alexi Natchev
Gerhard is excited and can hardly wait for Christmas day. His parents understand and set out to help him make the wait more pleasant and meaningful. Using this book, children can make Lebkuchen cookies and create their own Advent calendar in true German style . . . with cookies!

An Island Christmas
Written by Lynn Joseph/Illustrated by Catherine Stock
When you live on an island, the first day of the Christmas holiday must surely mean playing on the beach and in the waves. But, no, Mama says. There is too much to do: making sorrel, black currant cakes, aloe pies, soursop ice cream; having Christmas parades; decorating the Christmas tree; and wrapping and hiding presents. A real holiday treat, this book includes a note at the end about the islands in the southern Caribbean Sea and the traditions and cultural recipes mentioned in the book.

Nine Days to Christmas
Written by Marie Hall Ets/Illustrated by Aurora Labastida
This story explores a Mexican family's preparation for the annual Posadas—nine nights of celebration before Christmas. This year little Ceci gets to stay awake for the posadas, and have her own piñata and go on a special shopping trip with her mother to the old Mexican marketplace. The ending is lovely and especially endearing as it centers on little Ceci's star piñata and the Christmas star. Look carefully for this beautiful out-of-print book and join this family during a wonderful time of year. There are so many trails your family can take with this book as guide. Have your own *Posadas* celebration—this book shows you how!

A Kenya Christmas
Written by Tony Johnston/Illustrated by Leonard Jenkins
When Aunt Aida visits, she brings Christmas with her. Juma and Aunt Aida contrive to bring Father Christmas to the whole village using the chicken man, an elephant, and chicken feathers in a sack to serve as snow. Snow in Kenya! Join Juma's family in the country of Kenya to see how Christmas is celebrated in this part of Africia.

~ Older Children ~

✷A Christmas Memory
Written by Truman Capote/ Illustrated by Beth Peck or Lisbeth Zwerger
This story is as rich as the fruitcake that the two friends mix and make to give as Christmas gifts. The seven-year-old boy and the elderly lady with "shorn white hair" are an interesting pair of friends. But the message in this tale, which focuses on loneliness and acceptance, challenges us with a broader definition of friendship during a season when friendships are valued the most.

✷ The Trees Kneel at Christmas
Written by Maud Hart Lovelace
Everyone loves a miracle at Christmas time—and that is exactly what Afify and her little brother hope to see on Christmas. Having heard an old legend about trees kneeling in homage on Christmas Eve night, these two Lebanese children are determined to go to the Brooklyn Park to see it for themselves. This book is beautifully written, the prose is as special as Christmas itself.

✴ *The Gift of the Magi*
Written by O. Henry/Various Illustrators
This touching story tells of a newly married young couple who do not have money for Christmas gifts to give each other, so they sell the thing they love the most to find a gift of greater worth. This is one of those stories read to me when I was a child of four that I well remember and love today at forty. A classic.

The Silver Donkey
Written by Sonya Hartnett/ Illustrated by Don Powers
A blind soldier and his tiny silver donkey charm carry us into a mythical tale of heartbreak, horror, war, and hope. With the help of some children who find the solider lost, hungry, wet in the woods—and miles from home—the soldier shares with them several tales starring the donkey, the beast of burden, as the central character. While only the first tale concerns the Nativity, this book is a holiday classic because it highlights the beauty of humanity—the lovely things we are capable of, even amid tough circumstances. This book will reward all children who read it.

The Christmas Doll
Written by Elvira Woodruff/ Illustrated by Barbara Mcclintock
Reminiscent of the *Lost Doll* poem, this is a tale about two sisters trying to make it in a world of poverty, illness, and misfortune. Their luck seems to change when Miss Thimblebee hires Lucy to sew the famous Thimblebee hearts on her dolls. Soon Lucy learns what the wisest and oldest poets have always told us, "that the true miracle of Christmas is not in the getting, but in the giving." This book is full of hearts and warmth and Christmas meaning. Girls will love this profound tale about the true meaning of the holidays.

~ Just for Fun ~

The Mouse before Christmas
Written and Illustrated by Michael Garland
Remember the mouse who wasn't stirring in Clement Moore's version of *The Night before Christmas*? Well, this little mouse is "stirring and whirling all through the house." Being a curious little rodent, this mouse finds himself in Santa's bag and ends up going for a ride around the world. What I love about this book are the "monumental" sights the little mouse sees as they pass through various countries: Holland, Egypt, Italy, France, and the United States.

Bear Stays Up for Christmas
Written by Karma Wilson/ Illustrated by Jane Chapman
With the help of his friends, Bear stays up for all the Christmas preparations, feasting, and tree trimming. Then, after all his little forest friends fall asleep, Bear prepares to give them a Christmas surprise on Christmas morning: and what a joyful morning it is! Then his friends present him with a gift—a quilt that's actually big enough for him—and Bear is left to cover up and go into his hibernation sleep. Definitely fun for parent and child to read together.

Featured Selections

A Reflection on Sharing Books with Children at Christmas

By Elizabeth Foss

I can't remember what the first title was. But I remember the year. Michael, my firstborn, was just a baby and we sat down and paged through a Christmas picture book. I had an idea, as we sat there snuggled in the glow of the Christmas tree, and I was determined to bring the idea to life. Every year, we would add a book to our collection of Christmas stories. And every Advent, we'd retrieve the books from the storage box and put them in a basket by the tree to be read throughout the Advent and Christmas season.

And so, I asked family and friends for books as Christmas gifts. My criteria for selection were simple: the book had to have excellent prose or poetry and beautiful

pictures, and it had to be a book that begged an adult to read it. I wanted books of such high quality that we would both look eagerly towards this tradition every year. That first year, there were a few books in a basket—the start of a simple family joy.

I remember the first year my second son celebrated Christmas. Michael had long since memorized *Who Is Coming to Our House?* and he "read" it again and again to his little brother. The tradition had begun.

Around that time, the books began to take on a life of their own. We started referring to ourselves as the Kitchen Angels (from Tomie dePaola's *Country Angel Christmas*) as we began our seasonal baking. We made the star cookies featured in the story *Jingle the Christmas Clown*. We went to visit a live stable. We wrote special Christmas letters to mothers we loved and illustrated them in the style of Barbara Helen Berger's *The Donkey's Dream*. The books had come alive.

The little storage box is now two big plastic tubs. The basket under the tree is one of four baskets in our house. And, the books now tell the story of our family: *This is the Star* and *When It Snowed that Night* are inscribed to Patrick on the occasion of his Advent baptism. *Waiting for Noel* and *All for the Newborn Baby* are clearly Nicholas' and bring back fond memories of the year God blessed us with a Christmas baby of our very own. Among Mary Beth's books are the *The Legend of the Christmas Rose* and *Mary, The Mother of God*. Stephen looks forward to the day after Christmas and the family reading of *Stephen's Feast*. The illustration on the cover of *The Christmas Miracle of Jonathon Toomey* will always remind me of Michael at seven, the Advent he received the book as a gift for his First Holy Communion.

There are other boxes that contain our family Advent and Christmas treasures and the legacy of the books is there as well. Laminated pictures of the nativity, laced with gold in the style of Brian Wildsmith's *A Christmas Story* are nestled with poinsettia fairy doll ornaments inspired by *The Legend of the Poinsettia*. A handwritten icon of St. Nicholas brings back sweet memories of "mommy's favorite," *The Miracle of Saint Nicholas.*

More than any other family tradition at any other season, this tradition of reading and then living Advent and Christmas gifts is *ours*. I have been blessed with the opportunity to share our books and the ideas that go with them through columns and email correspondences and blog posts for over fifteen years. I know that living picture books take on a life of their own in many, many homes during Advent and Christmas.

Like no other season, this one inspires artists and writers to touch the hearts of children. I so treasure my boxes of Christmas books because I treasure the memory of the time I've spent sharing them with my children. And I look forward fondly to many, many more moments reading by the light of the tree with my own sweet angels—and with their children, too.

~ Advent Week One ~

Advent
Decoration and Preparation Stories

Sean Fitzpatrick , 2007

The Holly and the Ivy

The holly and the ivy,
Now are both well grown.
Of all the trees that are in the wood
The holly bears the crown.

The holly bears a blossom
As white as the lily flower,
And Mary bore sweet Jesus Christ
To be our sweet Saviour.

The holly bears a berry
As red as any blood,
And Mary bore sweet Jesus Christ
To do poor sinners good.

The holly bears a prickle
As sharp as any thorn,
And Mary bore sweet Jesus Christ
On Christmas Day in the morn.

The holly bears a bark
As bitter as any gall,
And Mary bore sweet Jesus Christ
For to redeem us all.

The holly and the ivy
Now are both well grown,
Of all the trees that are in the wood
The holly bears the crown.

—Traditional

A Reflection on Decoration
"A Window in Time"
By Alice Gunther

My young husband was learning all about married life when he found himself inside a Christmas Shop in Mystic, Connecticut on a warm August afternoon. He had left behind the rugged Seaport Museum not a quarter of an hour before and was following his feminine half up and down aisles of angels and glass balls, wondering, I am sure, how his luck could have turned around so quickly.

Before long, he heard me gasp, a sound he would get to know all too well in the months and years to come. If my father could have warned him about the import of that particular gasp, he probably would have said, not without some sympathy, "Alice saw something she *simply must* have."

It was a doll-sized Christmas bay window, hand wrought in cherry and beveled glass, bright and beaming as a page out of Hans Christian Anderson and arrayed in shades of green and gold and scarlet. Although it held no particular attraction for the twenty-six year old man by my side, he waited patiently as I inquired about the price. Seventy-five dollars. Far beyond anything we had to spend on a Christmas decoration in August, no matter how unique. I listened as the woman behind the counter spoke of the artist who created it, the sturdy workmanship, and the time and care taken to craft it. For seventy-five dollars though, it would never grace our cozy apartment, casting its expensive glow over the Nativity and collection of standing angels.

Days later, my mother called to ask about our weekend in Mystic. I told her of the clam chowder and clipper ships, a wooden church and the Christmas shop, mentioning the beautiful bay window wistfully, describing its beveled glass and bright green wreath.

Christmas rolled around that year, as Christmas always does, and before long we were sitting in my parents' living room exchanging presents. My father stroked a pair of plaid pajamas, and my mother spritzed a bit of perfume on her wrist, drinking in the fragrance with exclamations of delight. Their recently acquired son-in-law looked handsome in a new, green wool sweater, and I opened an oversized gift with interest.

As the paper fell away, there, to my delight and amazement, was the almost forgotten bay window, one of a kind and straight from the shop in Mystic. For once, I was speechless and looked up first at my mother, then my father, and then my dear young husband. My father's voice boomed out merrily, cushioned by laughter all around, "Your mother brought me on what I thought would be a fool's errand, but we found it!" My parents took turns telling the tale of how they drove three hours to Mystic without even knowing the name of the shop or its location. Once in town, they cruised up and down Main Street looking for sign of a Christmas Shop, but found none. It was only after lunch and a quick stop in an Antique store that they stumbled upon it by chance down a quiet side street. My mother described the bay window to the shopkeeper who had it wrapped for them in minutes.

Looking back on it, this type of thing was so typical of my parents. My mother, in particular, understood the importance of preparing for Our Savior's Birth with bright and thoughtful touches throughout the house. My heart still throbs to see her fat red candle lit to welcome the newborn king, the glorious Nativity scene outside the door, and her statue of the Christ Child—never gracing the front window until we returned from church on Christmas Eve. It was my mother who began my collection of angels after hearing her then teenage daughter muse about how the perfect Christmas tree should be "covered with angels." Thanks to her, opening our decorations each year is like turning the pages of a scrapbook—a timeless reminder of the important events of life and the happy, holy home my parents made together.

The gratitude in my heart for my parents' heartfelt gift has never faded all these years, especially as I look back upon the care and trouble and love it took to put it under the tree so long ago. Sometimes, if I find myself alone, with the tree shining brightly and the Christmas Bay Window burning its cheery glow, I seem to see through its beveled panes the happy light of Christmases long past. The scenes are set before me like the banquet in the Anderson tale, vivid and fleeting and warming to the core.

Nowadays, decorating and preparing the house for Christmas is especially joyful, because we have seven young and enthusiastic helpers, all of whom have inherited their mother and grandmother's penchant for wreaths and ribbons, angels and ornaments. Each year the children look forward to creating something new to add to Grandma's collection. To be just right for Grandma, the crafts must be religious, attractive, and simple enough for even the younger members of the family.

This year, the children made Madonna and Child ornaments, and I wish you could have seen the look on their grandmother's face when she opened her presents. Here are the simple steps involved, but be warned, your children will want to make them by the dozen. Fortunately, they are so inexpensive; you can encourage them to do just that.

Materials:
 Stiff paper or cardstock, preferably in shades of red, burgundy or green
Old Christmas cards with religious images
Optional: glitter, jewels, paint
Ribbon for hanging

Steps:
1. Twist a cone out of colored cardstock, stapling or hot gluing to secure. If you are planning to stand the image on a table, trim the edge of the cone to make it steady and even. (Figure 1.)
2. Cut out the loveliest Christmas card image possible. Each year, we try to set aside our favorite images for crafting the following Christmas. (Figure 2.)
3. Standing the cone point upright (like a steeple), glue the religious image to the front, wrapping it around at the bottom, but leaving the top to stand upright, creating a slightly three-dimensional effect. (Figure 3.)

This eye-catching ornament is perfect for sitting on the mantle, topping small trees and bedposts or hanging from a ribbon. Best of all, one or more may be made in a family assembly line, with Mom twisting the cones, older children affixing images, and the little ones decorating with glitter and jewels. As a finishing touch, the whole family can autograph and date the inside for Grandma, saying a prayer together for her special intention.

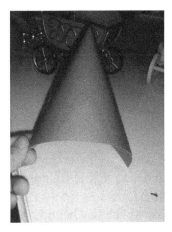

Figure 1.

Figure 2.

Figure 3.

The Legend of Tinsel Upon the Tree

In most people's minds, spiders are stereotyped as a Halloween symbol rather than a Christmas symbol. In their dark solitary habitats and hermit-like entrapments, these leggy, spindly creatures seem out of place in a brightly lit picturesque Christmas setting.

Yet let's stop and think about some spiders that we know and love through the virtual strands spun in storybooks. There are certain arachnids that have become very dear to us. Wilbur's spider friend in *Charlotte's Web* taught many of us what true friendship is. Miss Spider in *James and the Giant Peace* was a tender foster mother to James. Her presence assured us that nothing bad would happen to James as long as she was around. And, tell me, didn't you feel Miss Spider's grief as she told James about the fate of her grandmother when she stepped in wet paint and stuck to Aunt Spiker and Aunt Sponge's kitchen ceiling?

David Kirk has introduced us all to another lady spider that gives lovely tea parties and loves children in *Miss Spider's Tea Party*. And in *Sophie's Masterpiece* by Eileen Spinelli, with wonderful still-life pictures by Jane Dyer, we meet dear Sophie: an ordinary house spider who happens to be a French artist. While living in a world that does not accept Sophie because of what she is; she begins to spin a soft-spun blanket for a newborn baby who will find no warmth in the world she has been born into. Into this cloth, Sophie weaves her own artwork and it becomes a thing of beauty alive with starlight bright, pine-scented boughs, whispered lullabies, silky snowflakes, and Sophie's giving, humble heart.

All these portrayals of spiders take an otherwise drab existence and turn it into something translucently beautiful and glittering, all through the power of a storybook.

Rowena Bennett wrote a poem about some house spiders who had hoped to get a glimpse of the Christmas tree from the rafters up above but, the day before Christmas, the housemaid sweeps them out the door. On a winter's night out in the snow the spiders weep for not being part of the Christmas celebration. And:

> *The fairies said: "Each living thing*
> *that creeps, or crawls, or flaps a wing*
> *shall share the birthday of the King."*

They bid the spiders into the parlor to see the Christmas tree and, because they are so small, are placed upon the tree branches so they can see, and smell, and feel the magic of Christmas. Then they thank the kind fairies and creep back into their secluded cracks to sleep until the morn. But the tree is now huddled in the gray webs that trailed behind the little spiders and the fairies know that the little children will be sadly disappointed to see their beautiful tree dull and dreary on Christmas morning. So, the fairies wave their fairy wands and . . .

You'll have to read the poem to see what happens.

Golden Cobwebs

(An Old Tale Retold in Verse)

The Christmas tree stood by the parlor door,
But the parlor door was locked
And the children could not get inside
Even though they knocked.
For a Christmas tree must wait, folks say,
And not be seen till Christmas Day.
But the cat had seen the Christmas tree
As she prowled the house by night,

And the dog had seen the Christmas tree
By the moon's enchanting light;
And a little mouse beside her hole
Had looked at it with eyes of coal.
Even the spiders hoped to see
The secret, silent Christmas tree.

They planned, one day, to creep and crawl
Out of their cracks and up the wall
To get the highest view of all.
But just that day with mop and broom
The housemaid swept them from the room
And so the spiders could not see
The secret, silent Christmas tree.

The fairies heard the spiders weep,
All on a winter's night,
Although their cries made softer sounds
Than moth wings make in flight.
The fairies said: "Each living thing
That creeps, or crawls, or flaps a wing
Shall share the birthday of the King."

They took the spiders to the tree
And, since they were too small
To see as far as cat or mouse,
The fairies let them crawl
Along each twig and bending branch
To look at every ball
And silver star and popcorn string;
And when they had seen everything

They thanked the fairies and went back
Each one to sleep inside his crack.
But, oh, the tree when they were gone
Was very sad to look upon!
Its branches were more gray than green
And little webs hung in between
That dulled the lights and all the sheen.

The fairies shook their heads and sighed,
For in their wisdom, ever wide,
They knew no housewife cared to see
Dull cobwebs on a Christmas tree.
They knew the children, too, would weep
To waken from their yuletide sleep
And glimpse a tree all bearded gray
That would not shine on Christmas Day....

And so they turned the webs to gold
By waving fairy wands, I'm told;
And that is why there'll always be
Bright cobwebs on a Christmas tree.
—Rowena Bennett

There are three children's books about spiders beautifying Christmas trees with their cobwebs featured in this study guide. Each one gives a different "spin" on the story of the origin of the tradition of tinsel on the tree. I was hesitant to introduce either book because most children don't like spiders, including mine, and I was worried spiders at Christmas time would not be well-received. Yet I personally liked the books and my children did as well.

I hope you enjoy this nostalgic piece about the origin of tinsel and remember our spider friends whenever you see shining tinsel upon the Christmas tree. I know you'll think of them when it's time to take the sticky tinsel off the tree.

The Christmas Cobwebs
Written by Odds Bodkin/ Illustrated by Terry Widener
Published by Gulliver Books, Harcourt, Inc., 2001.
Illustrations copyright © Terry Widener, reprinted by permission of the publisher.

Vocabulary
humble   cobbler   growled   miraculous   trudge   abandon

Discussion Questions
1. Where had the cobbler come from?
2. What did he and his wife bring with them to remind them of Germany?
3. What was in the box? What were they made of?
4. What happened during the night and what did the cobbler save?
5. Where did they go?
6. Why didn't the wife sweep away the cobwebs in the little shack?
7. Why did the cobbler say that?
8. What did the cobbler do with the ornaments? Why?
9. What was more precious than the ornaments?
10. Describe what happened that night?

Copywork

"But we have something much more precious. We have each
other. And look and see how beautiful our tree is."
                        —words of Papa in *The Christmas Cobwebs*

Parent's Help Page
(*The Christmas Cobwebs*)

Observation
1. How were the precious keepsake ornaments from Germany and the delicate ornaments made by the spiders the same yet different?
2. Compare the ornaments in the story with your own ornaments. You might want to take out your ornaments and look them over in anticipation of decorating the tree. Do you have any ornaments similar to those in the story? Do you have any very special ornaments that have a special story behind them. Talk about the stories of how you acquired the different ornaments you own.

Discussion Answers
1. The cobbler came from Germany.
2. The cobbler and his wife brought with them a carved oak box.
3. Christmas tree ornaments lay in the box. They were made of blown-glass.
4. During the night, their house caught on fire. The cobbler saved the box of ornaments.
5. They moved into an abandoned farmer's shack.
6. The wife left the cobwebs alone because her husband told her, "Please don't take their homes."
7. Because the family had lost their home and he felt sorry for the spiders.
8. The cobbler sold the ornaments. He needed the money to buy tools and leather to make shoes so he could provide for his family.
9. The cobbler's family was more precious than the ornaments and they still had each other.
10. That night the spiders dropped down onto the Christmas tree and wove beautiful Christmas ornaments onto it.

Enrichment Activity
1. Try to create some ornaments like the ones the spiders made. Use silver or white chenille stems (aka pipe cleaners) and form into various shapes. You can attach several of them together at right angles to make a snowflake-type of ornament. Experiment with them and see what you can create!
2. Begin an ornament keepsake tradition with your children. You can collect fine ornaments for each child and keep them in a box marked with their names to give them when they someday "leave" home. OR, as a family you can make one new special ornament for each child each year. Every year you can take out the previous years' ornaments and talk about how you made them, what happened that year, and so on.

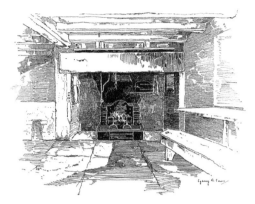

The Cobweb Christmas
Written by Shirley Climo/ Illustrated by Joe Lasker
Published by Thomas Y. Crowell, 1982.

Vocabulary

soot   curtsey   sprout   garlands   sprig   skitter

Discussion Questions

1. What does the word Tante mean in German?
2. Was the old woman happy? How do you know?
3. Why was the cottage untidy?
4. How did Tante "fetch" Christmas?
5. How did Tante "make" Christmas?
6. What did she make sure was on her Christmas tree?
7. What was the only creature that did not have anything on the tree?
8. Who was Christkindel?
9. What did Tante want more than anything?
10. Who let the spiders into Tante's cottage?
11. What did the spiders want to see?
12. What did the spiders do to the tree?
13. Was the tree pretty after the spiders spun their webs upon it? What gift did Christkindel leave for Tante?
14. What did Tante change after seeing her Cobweb Christmas?

Copywork

> Time to clean for Christmas.
> Time to fetch Christmas.
> Time to make Christmas.
> Time to share Christmas.
> Time to wait for Christmas.
> Time for Christmas magic.
> —Tante in *The Cobweb Christmas*

Parent's Help Page
(*The Cobweb Christmas*)

Observation

Name the items Tante had that kept her happy:
- A canary for singing
- A cat for purring
- A dog to doze beside the fire
- A donkey for riding
- A cow and a goat for milk and cheese
- A rooster to crow her out of bed
- A hen to lay an egg for her breakfast

Name the items that Tante put on her Christmas tree:
- Cookies (gingerbread, almond, cinnamon) and apples for the children.
- A bone for the dog
- A sprig of catnip for the cat
- Bits of cheese into pinecones for the mice
- Bundles of oats for the donkey, cow, and goat
- Nuts for the squirrels
- Garland of seeds for the birds
- Cracked corn for the chickens

Discussion Answers

1. Tante means "Auntie" in German.
2. Yes, the old woman was happy. You can tell because the story says that her cottage "suited the old woman."
3. The cottage was untidy because Tante had so many animals.
4. Tante "fetched" Christmas by going to look for the perfect Christmas tree.
5. Tante "made" Christmas by decorating the tree.
6. She made sure there was "something for everyone" on her Christmas tree.
7. The spiders.
8. Christkindel was the spirit who visited the children on Christmas Eve and left them presents.
9. Tante wanted "some Christmas magic that was not of her own making."
10. Christkindel let the spiders into the cottage.
11. The spiders wanted to see Tante's Christmas tree.
12. The spiders left their spider webs upon the tree.
13. No, the tree was not pretty. Christkindel touched the spider webs and turned them into threads of silver and gold.
14. Tante left some spiders on her ceiling to "share Christmas" with her and sprinkled tinsel over her tree to remind her of Cobweb Christmas.

Enrichment Activity

1. The spiders come "creeping, crawling, sneaking softly, scurrying, hurrying, quickly, lightly, zipping, zagging, weaving, and wobbling…" into the cottage. Your children can act out each of the verbs. Think of the other animals with whom Tante shared her Christmas. Your child can you act out the way they moved and think of action verbs to describe their movements.

2. Have your child look over his copywork and write down what he did to make each thing happen. Decorate the page with Christmas stickers.

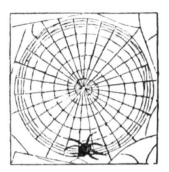

The Cobweb Curtain
Written by Jenny Koralek/Illustrated by Pauline Baynes
Published by Henry Holt and Co., 1989.

Vocabulary

clumsy   dwell   snatch   clatter   jeer

Discussion Questions

1. What kept the Christ child warm?
2. Who stopped the wise men at the city's gate and what did he ask them?
3. Did the wise men tell the messenger where the Christ child was?
4. Who overheard them talking? Why was he afraid for the family?
5. What did the shepherd do?
6. Who was outside the cave and heard them?
7. What did the spider do and why?
8. Why did the soldiers not check the cave?
9. Do you think the spider's web was more precious than gold, herbs, and perfume? Why?
10. What did the shepherd do with the spider's web?
11. What would the frosty web on a tree remind the shepherd's family of each year?

Copywork

> So He has come at last, and for that I am glad. But had I saved the life
> of any child, I would still be happy.
>
> —The spider in *The Cobweb Curtain*

Parent's Help Page
(*The Cobweb Curtain*)

Discussion Answers
1. The animals' furry bodies and steamy breath.
2. A messenger stopped the wise men and asked them if the baby they had bowed to was a king.
3. No, they did not tell the messenger where the Christ child was.
4. A young shepherd heard the conversation between the wise men and the messenger. He feared the Christ child was in danger because the king would be jealous.
5. The shepherd told them the child was in danger and took them to a dark cave to hide.
6. A spider was outside the cave.
7. The spider spun a web across the entrance to the cave to keep the family warm.
8. Because the web was frosted and frozen, the soldier thought it had been there for many days.
9. The spider's web was more precious because it saved the life of the Christ child.
10. The shepherd took the frosty web and put it on a small tree.
11. The web on the tree would remind the shepherd's family of the Christ child's birthday and the gift of the spider.

Enrichment Activity
1. On a sheet of construction paper, make your own spider web. Use glue to make several circles within a circle. Take a toothpick and run through the glue in all directions. Add silver glitter or snowy white glitter to glue and wait for it to dry. Add star stickers over the rest of the paper to show a starry sky. Attach a plastic spider to your picture if you wish.
2. This recipe is known by many names and is done in many ways. It is an easy one to do with children.

Spider Cookies

Variation 1:
Submitted by Maria Cunningham
12 oz. bag of chocolate chips
12 oz. bag of butterscotch chips
6oz.bag of chow mein noodles
½ cup peanuts or cashews

Melt chips on low heat. Mix together. Remove from heat and stir in noodles and peanuts. Drop onto wax paper using a tablespoon. Let set for about 8 hours. Store in cool place. These can also be frozen.

Variation 2:
1 pkg. (12 oz.) chocolate chips
1 can (3 oz.) Chinese noodles
Melt chocolate in double boiler top. Remove from heat. Gradually add Chinese noodles, as much as mixture will hold. Drop by globs on wax paper. Cool and store (or eat).

Variation 3:
2 cups semisweet chocolate chips, divided
1/2 cup crispy rice cereal
1/4 cup sweetened shredded coconut
1-1/2 cup chow mein noodles
1 small tube white decorator frosting

Melt one cup of chocolate chips in a heavy saucepan over low heat until melted. (Or, melt in the microwave by placing chocolate chips in a 2 to 4 cup glass measure. Heat on high in the microwave for 1 minute. Remove, stir, and heat on high for 1 minute longer. Let set for 1 minute and stir until chips are melted.) Mix in the cereal and the coconut. Drop by teaspoonfuls onto waxed paper for the spider bodies. Melt the second cup of chocolate chips. Gently stir in chow mein noodles (being careful not to break noodles up). Pick noodles out one by one and attach them to the spider bodies for legs (8 to a spider, of course). Add bits of frosting for eyes.

Waiting for Christmas
Written by Kathleen Long Bostrom/ Illustrated by Alexi Natchev
Published by Zonderkidz, 2006.

Discussion Questions
1. Gerhard is excited about Christmas. How does his mother tell him to wait?
2. Gerhard's father tells him that a special baby had to wait for his first Christmas gifts as well. Who was that baby?
3. What were Jesus' first Christmas gifts? Who brought them?
4. Did the three kings bring the gifts to Jesus on the night he was born?
5. What is Lebkuchen?
6. What was the chalk for?
7. What kind of Advent Calendar did Gerhard's mother make for him?
8. When Gerhard prayed, what did he ask God to help him be? Do you think that was a good prayer? Explain.

Copywork

Good things are worth waiting for.
—Mama in *Waiting for Christmas*

Parent's Help Page
(Waiting for Christmas)

Discussion Answers
1. She tells him that the best way is to keep busy.
2. The baby was Jesus.
3. Jesus' first Christmas gifts were gold, frankincense, and myrrh. The three kings brought the gifts.
4. No. It was two or three years later.
5. Lebkuchen is a special Christmas cookie.
6. The chalk was for Gerhard to draw twenty-four lines on the door. Gerhard could erase one line each night until they were all gone.
7. Gerhard's mother made him a cookie calendar.
8. Gerhard asked God to help him be more patient.

Enrichment Activities
1. Advent Calendars are a joy to have during the Advent season:
   - You can buy an Advent Calendar in a store.
   - Look in *Waiting for Christmas* for ideas. The book includes a nice poster calendar in the back with numerical stickers to keep track of the days before Christmas.
   - You can also create your own cookie Advent Calendar.
   - Another simple idea is to take a ribbon and hot glue twenty-four pieces of gum or candy on the ribbon. Each day of Advent is observed when you remove one piece of gum or candy from the ribbon.
   - You can add one piece to your nativity scene each day. Have the pieces sitting on a shelf with the day's number written on it. On that day, ceremoniously place the piece in the manger scene and talk about it.

2. You can make the special cookie mentioned in this story using the following recipe:

Lebkuchen Recipe
Contributed by Cay Gibson

3 cups all-purpose flour
$\frac{1}{2}$ cup honey
$1\frac{1}{2}$ teaspoon ground nutmeg
$\frac{1}{2}$ cup dark molasses
$1\frac{1}{2}$ teaspoon ground cinnamon
$\frac{1}{2}$ cup thinly sliced almonds
$\frac{1}{2}$ teaspoon baking soda
$\frac{1}{2}$ cup of candied cherries, pineapple, and orange peels (chopped very fine)
$\frac{1}{2}$ teaspoons ground cloves
$\frac{1}{2}$ teaspoon ground allspice

Lemon Glaze (optional)
1 Egg
$\frac{3}{4}$ cup brown sugar
1 T. lemon juice

Instructions:
In a bowl stir together the flour, nutmeg, cinnamon, soda, cloves and allspice. In a larger mixing bowl, beat the egg until fluffy. Slowly add the brown sugar. Stir in honey and molasses. Add dry ingredients to molasses mixture; beat until the mixture is well combined. Stir in almonds, candied fruits, and peels. Cover mixing bowl and chill in refrigerator for several hours.

On floured surface, roll dough into a large square. Cut into good size rectangles. Place cookies on greased cookie sheet at least two inches apart. Bake at 375° for twelve minutes or until done. Cool cookies for about one minute before removing to wire rack. While cookies are warm, brush with the Lemon Glaze, if desired.

Note: I would brush with Lemon Glaze the last five minutes of baking due to the raw egg.

That Holy Thing

They all were looking for a king
To slay their foes and lift them high:
Thou cam'st, a little baby thing
That made a woman cry.

O Son of Man, to right my lot
Naught but Thy presence can avail;
Yet on the road Thy wheels are not,
Nor on the sea Thy sail!

My how or when Thou wilt not heed,
But come down thine own secret stair,
That Thou mayst answer all my need--
Yea, every bygone prayer.
                              —George MacDonald

The Twenty-Four Days before Christmas

by Madeleine L'Engle/Illustrated by Joe DeVelasco

Here is an activity to do each day of December that corresponds with the activities of the family in the book. You could read the book all at once to you children early in Advent, or read a few chapters each night the first week.

December 1: Give each child a blank December calendar—each day they are to list something they like about Christmas. An Advent Calendar with small windows to open is always nice. Serve pancakes with applesauce and syrup and hot chocolate.

December 2: Make fun Christmas shapes from cookie dough (snowmen are easy!). Eat cookies with apple cider. Read *The Baker's Dozen* by Heather Forest and illustrated by Susan Gaber.

December 3: Use construction paper, cardstock or Christmas cards for Christmas symbols. Have children create their own or find Christmas symbols in a magazine to cut out. Hang symbols from a clothes hanger trimmed with Christmas ribbons.

December 4: Make stars out of popsicle sticks. Decorate with gold or silver glitter glue. Read *This is the Star* by Joyce Dunbar and illustrated by Gary Blythe. Eat popsicles first!

December 5: Read the story of *The Elves and the Shoemaker* by Paul Galdone. Have the children leave their shoes in the hallway or outside their bedroom door for treats and gold coins from St. Nicholas. Serve a "Poor Man's Stew" with this story!

December 6: Feast Day of St. Nicholas—Read the true story of the real Saint Nick. Look up St. Nicholas in an encyclopedia and write a one paragraph report on him. Illustrate your report. Read *The Baker's Dozen: A Saint Nicholas Tale* by Aaron Shepard and illustrated by Wendy Edelson. Bake and decorate gingerbread men.

December 7: Make an angel from an empty toilet paper roll and cotton balls. Read *Bright Christmas: An Angel Remembers* by Kate Kiesler.

December 8: Give your children a holiday mug filled with goodies. Drink hot cocoa or tea while listening to Christmas carols. Add a cinnamon stick to the holiday mug to stir their tea.

December 9: Make a rope of Christmas bells using a red ribbon and jingle bells. Use for decoration.

December 10: Read *Yes, Virginia, There is a Santa Claus—The Classic Edition* by Francis P. Church and illustrated by Joel Spector.

December 11: Use a wire-mesh 3-tiered fruit basket. Let children fill with beautiful shiny Christmas ornaments, fruit, and chocolates. Serve fruit and cinnamon/sugar toast for breakfast.

December 12: Make your favorite Christmas candy.

December 13: Make stuffed dates, candid figs, and sugared nuts. Enjoy eating them! Make a spiced fig cake and decorate it with sugared nuts!

December 14: Select the best-looking berries and pine needles from the woods to use in the Christmas Crèche. Read *Night Tree* by Eve Bunting. Bake a berry pie!

December 15: Adorn house and lawn with Christmas decorations and/or take a car drive to see the Christmas lights. Read *The Miracle of Saint Nicholas* by Gloria Whelan and illustrated by Judith Brown.

December 16: Decorate the front door with the Christmas wreath. Decorate the rest of house with mistletoe and holly.

December 17: Make Angel Cookies—use sugar cookie dough (large triangle for body/ circle for head/ semi-circles for wings.) Decorate with lovely candy sprinkles. YUM!

December 18: Give each child a special white candle. Allow them to decorate it with pretty beads and sequins. Read *The Light of Christmas* by Richard Paul Evans and illustrated by Daniel Craig/ Read *The Christmas Candle* by Richard Paul Evans and illustrated by Jacob Collins.

December 19: Make Christmas cards and a Christmas banner for the elderly in the nursing home and for local shut-ins.

December 20: Bring out the family crèche and read the Christmas story while displaying the crèche. Have the children take turns placing the nativity figures. Read *The Donkey's Dream* by Barbara Helen Berger. Make vanilla crepes with jellies/jams/marmalades for filling.

December 21: Decorate the Christmas Tree. Read *Why Christmas Trees Aren't Perfect* by Dick Schneider and illustrated by Elizabeth J. Miles. Read *The Tale of Three Trees* by Angela Elwell Hunt and illustrated by Tim Jonke. Serve buttered popcorn and Christmas chocolates!

December 22: Sing or listen to *Oh Come All Ye Faithful.* Make snowflake paper cut-outs and sprinkle with glitter for decoration. Serve hamburgers and milk shakes for dinner.

December 23: Attend a Christmas Play or watch *A Christmas Carol* or *It's a Wonderful Life/* Serve po-boy sandwiches!

December 24: Attend church services. Let each child light his/her Christmas candle. Read *Twas the Night Before Christmas* by Clement C. Moore and illustrated by Tasha Tudor (or your favorite illustrator).

December 25: Read your favorite nativity storybook in front of the crèche on Christmas morning. Have a Joyful and Blessed Christmas Day!

The Christmas Miracle of Jonathan Toomey
Written by Susan Wojciechowski/ Illustrated by P.J. Lynch

Image from The Christmas Miracle of Jonathan Toomey. Text© 1995 by Susan Wojciechowski.
Illustrations © 1995 P.J. Lynch. Reproduced be permission of the publisher, Candlewick Press, Inc.,
Cambridge, MA.

Vocabulary

bellow   gripe   strokes   shawl   embroider

Discussion Questions
1. Why do you think the village children called Mr. Jonathan Toomey, Mr. Gloomy?
2. What was Mr. Toomey's occupation?
3. What was the reason for Mr. Toomey's sadness? Does it seem like the village people know this?
4. Why did the widow come to his house one day early in December?
5. What did the Widow McDowell tell her son he could learn from Mr. Toomey?
6. Why do you think Mr. Toomey insists that the widow not sit in the rocking chair and is upset that she takes the tablecloth from the drawer?
7. What Christmas gifts did Widow McDowell and her son give Mr. Toomey?
8. How did Mr. Toomey finally get the image of Mary and Jesus right in the carving?
9. Who were the people in the picture that he took out of the drawer?
10. What was the miracle of Jonathan Toomey?

Copywork

> He unpacked Mary wearing a rough woolen shawl, looking down, loving her precious baby son. Jesus was smiling and reaching up to touch his mother's face.
> —From *The Christmas Miracle of Jonathan Toomey*

Parent's Help Page
(The Christmas Miracle of Jonathan Toomey)

Observation

1. After reading the description of Jonathan Toomey on the second page, have your child narrate back to you Mr. Toomey's appearance. Compare it to his appearance at the end of the story.
2. See if your child can link Mr. Toomey and his woodcarving to St. Joseph and his carpentry.
3. See if your child can remember how Thomas described the figures Mr. Toomey was carving:
    1. Sheep—happy
    2. Cow—proud
    3. Angel—important
    4. Wise men—wonderfully dressed
    5. St. Joseph—serious and protective
    6. Jesus—smiling
    7. Mary—loving

Discussion Answers

1. They called him Mr. Gloomy because he was a "gloomy" person and this rhymed nicely with Toomey. He seldom smiled and never laughed.
2. Mr. Toomey was a woodcarver.
3. Mr. Toomey was "gloomy" because his wife and baby had died some years earlier. The village people were not aware of this.
4. Widow McDowell and her son came to Mr. Toomey's house to order the carving of a set of nativity scene figures.
5. Widow McDowell told her son he could learn the "virtue of silence" from Mr. Toomey.
6. These are the things his wife used and his grief is too great to see them used.
7. The widow and her son gave Mr. Toomey the red scarf she had been knitting and the little wooden robin Thomas had carved out of pine.
8. He uses the picture that he took out of the drawer.
9. It is his wife and baby.
10. The miracle was Mr. Toomey letting go of his grief over loosing his wife and baby and being able to love others again.

Enrichment Activity

1. Get out your own box of Nativity figures and put on some soft religious Christmas music in the background. Sit and practice the "virtue of silence" and let the Christ child speak to your heart.

2. If you haven't already set up your manger scene, doing it now would be a nice connection with this story.

3. Make a batch of molasses cookies or raisin buns. (The widow brings Mr. Toomey these treats.)

Grandma Maher's Molasses Cookies
Contributed by Julie (Maher) Howard

$4 \frac{1}{2}$ cups Flour
$1 \frac{1}{3}$ cups Sugar
1 teaspoon Salt
2 teaspoons Baking Soda
2 teaspoons ground Cinnamon
2 teaspoons ground Ginger
1 cup shortening
1 cup molasses
4 eggs, well beaten
Additional Sugar

Blend dry ingredients. Blend in shortening and add molasses. Add eggs. Roll a teaspoon of dough in small bowl of white sugar. Place on greased cookie sheet and press cookie slightly. Bake at 350 degrees for 8-10 minutes.

*A Christmas Memory**
by Truman Capote/illustrated by Beth Peck

This story can be read by an older child on his or her own, or you can read it aloud to the whole family. There are several illustrated versions available through the library or local bookstore.

Vocabulary

inaugurating   dilapidated   skinflint
festooned   simultaneously   rime
cavort   squander   goad

Discussion Questions

1. Describe the old woman. What makes her special to the boy?
   Think of some of her behaviors that tell the reader about her character.
2. Do you think the other people in the house are nice to her? Explain.
3. Why do you think this story is such a strong memory for the boy?
4. Narrate or create a sequence of pictures to explain the steps the woman and the boy followed to make the fruitcake.
5. Think about the observation made by the old woman on Christmas day about seeing Jesus at the end of one's life. What does she mean by it? Do you agree with it? Explain.
6. Why are there two kites flying to the sky in the end?

Copywork

> I'll wager at the very end a body realizes the Lord has already shown Himself. That things as they are, just seeing what they've always seen, was seeing Him. As for me, I could leave the world with today in my eyes.
> —the old woman in *A Christmas Memory*

*Study guide contributed by Margot Davidson

Parent's Help Page
(*A Christmas Memory*)

Observation

1. Notice the author's writing style. He uses short incomplete sentences at various times in the book. Find some examples of this and notice what effect it has on the story telling.
2. Notice the similes in the story.
   a. *The black stove, stoked with coal and firewood, glows like a lighted pumpkin.*
   b. *. . . letting it loose like a kite on a broken string.*
   Work with your children on creating some similes to describe Christmas at your home.

Discussion Answers

1. Answers will vary. Allow the children to say what they think of the old woman and her relationship with the boy. Some behaviors they might mention are the routine of making the fruitcake every year and sending it to strangers, not telling the rich lady where she got the Christmas tree, making a kite for a Christmas present, etc.
2. The other people in the house aren't really nice to her. They seem to tolerate her but basically ignore her.
3. The woman was a dear friend, his only friend in an unfriendly place. She helped make Christmas special for him.
4. Step in making fruitcake: Collect the nuts and hull them, gathering money, buying the needed items (including the whiskey!), mix it, and bake. Then let it sit on sills and shelves. You may want to have your child name all the ingredients that go into their cake.
5. Answers will vary. Give the child time to think and form his thoughts about the quote. (Part of this scene is used as the copywork selection above.) Draw out his thought by asking questions about the answers he gives.
6. The two kites symbolize the souls of the boy and the old woman. The author uses this Imagery since they had made kites for each other. They go off into the sky because he has to let go of the nice time in his life when they were friends. That time goes off with her into the sky. The younger children may not get this imagery, so discuss and let it sink in.

Enrichment Activities

1. Your children can write about or draw their favorite Christmas memory. You might start a Christmas tradition of creating a memory book of each Christmas. On the last day of Christmas or just after Epiphany, have each child draw or write about his favorite part of that Christmas. Keep the books and bring them out each year to look over Christmases past.
2. Plan your Christmas breakfast menu with the children. Here is what the boy and the old woman had: flapjacks, fried squirrel, hominy grits and honey-in-the-comb.

3. Make some fruitcake using either of the recipes on the following pages. Be sure to start it early in the season so it has time to "ripen"! Or you can try the Fruitcake Cookies recipe available in the Recipe Appendix.

Variation 1
Contributed by Mary Gildersleeve

"I'm one of the few folks out there who *loves* fruitcake, especially if the fruit has been steeped in bourbon for a day or so! Here's the recipe (edited to suit us) from *A Continual Feast* by Evelyn Birge Vitz. I make this every year (and now the littles are helping too!)."

Black Fruitcake
"Here's the recipe (edited to suit us) from *A Continual Feast* by Evelyn Birge Vitz. I make this every year (and now the littles are helping too!)."

1 cup bourbon or Irish Whiskey (or fruit juice, if you'd rather)
$1\frac{1}{2}$ cups currants
$1\frac{1}{2}$ cups raisins
$1\frac{1}{2}$ cups golden raisins
$1\frac{1}{2}$ cups candied fruit peels
$\frac{1}{2}$ cup butter at room temp
$1\frac{1}{3}$ cups dark brown sugar
3 eggs
$\frac{3}{4}$ cup all purpose flour
$\frac{1}{2}$ cup whole wheat flour
$\frac{1}{4}$ tsp salt
1 tsp baking powder
1 tsp cinnamon
1 tsp ground ginger
$\frac{1}{2}$ tsp ground allspice
$\frac{1}{2}$ tsp ground nutmeg
$\frac{1}{2}$ tsp ground cloves
$\frac{1}{4}$ cup dark molasses
$\frac{1}{2}$ cup chopped, blanched almonds

Pour 1 cup of liquid over all the fruits—let steep for at least 6 hours (the night before you put together works really well). Drain the fruits and pat them dry. Reserve the liquid, adding more to make it equal a full 1 cup. This liquid helps plump the fruit and gives a wonderful flavor to the cake.

In a large bowl, cream the butter with the sugar until fluffy. Add the eggs, mixing thoroughly after each egg is added.

Dredge the fruits with $\frac{1}{4}$ cup of the flour. Sift the remaining the flour with the salt, baking powder and spices. Stir the molasses, liquid, nuts and flour alternately together with the dredged fruit and egg/sugar mix until you've got a nice mixed batter.

Grease with butter two 5x9 loaf pans or several smaller pans (about 6 small foil loaf pans). Grease liberally to ensure easy removal of cakes.

Plop batter into pans. Press the batter into the pans to ensure no air pockets -- use the back of a spoon. Bake at 275° for about 4 hours or until cakes test done (use a thin spaghetti noodle or straw to test). Smaller cakes take about an hour less. Cool in pans for 20 minutes then turn cakes out of pan and finish cooling on a rack. Wrap tightly in foil to preserve freshness and ENJOY!

Variation 2
Contributed by Lara Pennell

"I think what most American don't like about fruitcake is the citron and (to a lesser degree) the citrus peel. This recipe contains neither, but is very rich in nuts, something that American do like. I think that this is why these fruitcake recipes are successful on this side of the border. Citron and peel may be added for those who desire it by reducing some of the other candied fruits."

Sept-Isles Fruitcake
(It's the jam that makes this fruitcake unique and moist)
1 c raisins
1 c golden raisins
1 c currants
2 lb candied red and green cherries
1 c pecan halves
1 c chopped blanched almonds
$1 \frac{2}{3}$ c flour (divided)
$\frac{1}{2}$ c molasses
$\frac{2}{3}$ c strawberry jam
$\frac{1}{4}$ t baking soda
1 t each: cinnamon, allspice
$\frac{1}{4}$ t mace
$\frac{1}{4}$ t nutmeg
$\frac{2}{3}$ c butter
$\frac{2}{3}$ c brown sugar
4 eggs
3 T orange juice
$\frac{1}{2}$ c brandy, whiskey or rum (and more if you want to spoon it on as the cake ripens)

Combine fruit and nuts and $\frac{1}{3}$ c flour. Mix remaining dry ingredients. Cream butter, sugar. Add eggs. Add molasses, orange juice, brandy (or whiskey or rum), jam. Stir in fruit. Fold in flour-spice mixture $\frac{1}{3}$ at a time. Spoon into well greased, brown paper lined cheesecake pan. Bake at 250° 3-3 $\frac{1}{2}$ hours till it tests done. Put a pan of hot water in the oven to bake with the fruitcake to keep the baking environment moist. Let ripen at least 3 weeks wrapped in rum (or brandy or whiskey) soaked cheesecloth or tea towel and then wrapped in foil or plastic. Add liquor as desired.

~ Advent Week Two ~

Giving
St. Nicholas
Santa Claus

Sean Fitzpatrck,© 2007

The Joy of Giving

Somehow, not only for Christmas
  But all the long year through,
The joy that you give to others
  Is the joy that comes back to you;
And the more you spend in blessing
  The poor and lonely and sad,
The more of your heart's possessing
  Returns to make you glad.
                    —John Greenleaf Whittier

The Christmas Coat
Written by Clyde Robert Bulla/ Illustrated by Sylvie Wickstrom
Published by Alfred A. Knopf, 1989

Discussion Questions

1. Why did Mama have to work so hard? Did she feel like a brave woman? How do you know?
2. Were they a happy family? How can you tell?
3. What was Mama's one wish?
4. Why did Mama draw a chalk line across the floor? Do you think it will work? Explain.
5. What did the boys begin to argue about one day? What were they going to buy her?
6. What happened to the coat that the boys found on the table and what did the boys do with it?
7. Who was the coat for?
8. What did the boys decide to do about the torn coat?
9. How did the boys pay for the repaired coat?
10. Do you think they should they have told their Mama what happened to the coat? Why didn't they tell her?
11. After giving the tailor their Christmas money, what did the boys give their Mama for Christmas?
12. What was the real gift they gave Mama that made her so happy?

Copywork

Blessed is the servant who loves his brother as much when he is sick and useless as when he is well and an be of service to him. And blessed is he who loves his brother as well when he is afar off as when he is by his side, and who would say nothing behind his back he might not, in love, say before his face.

—St Francis of Assisi

When brothers agree, no fortress is so strong as their common life.
—Antisthenes

Parent's Help Page
(*The Christmas Coat*)

Discussion Answers

1. Mama had to work hard because Papa had gone to war and never come back. She had to work to provide for the boys and did not feel brave at all. She often wanted to sit down and cry.
2. No, the boys quarreled and fought.
3. Mama wished the boys could be good for just one day.
4. She was tired of all their fighting and wanted to separate them. Let the child predict whether it will work or not.
5. The boys began to argue about who would buy the better gift for Mama. Hans was going to buy her a gold comb with diamonds in it. Otto was going to buy her a handkerchief with strawberries embroidered on it.
6. The boys fought over the coat and tore it in half, and then they put it back into the box without telling Mama what they had done.
7. The coat was for Karl, a sick little neighbor boy.
8. They took the coat back to the tailor to see if he could fix it.
9. The boys put their Christmas money together to pay for the coat.
10. Answers will vary. Let you child discuss the behavior.
11. The boys gave their mother an invisible comb with diamonds in it and a make-believe handkerchief with strawberries.
12. They had given her what she had wished for. They were good—not just one day but—for two days.

Enrichment Activity

1. Ask your child to think about his/her relationship with their own siblings. Are they ever like Hans and Otto? What lesson did they learn from the story *The Christmas Coat*?
2. Draw an outline of a coat, or of a Christmas tree. Have each child write what he would give his brothers and sisters if he could.
3. After reading this book, it might be a good time to start the tradition of a"Kris Kringle" exchange among the siblings. Each name goes in a hat and each person draws a name. In the remaining days before Christmas, each child works secretly to do nice things for the person whose name he drew and each child makes a gift for that person. Kris Kringles are revealed and gifts exchanged on Christmas morning or the morning of the Epiphany.

The Christmas Candle
by Richard Paul Evans/ Jacob Collins
Published by Simon & Schuster Children's Publishing Division, 1998.

Vocabulary

hearth	chandler	sculptor	sprites	coppers
illumination	pence	contempt	prank	peculiar
clump	awning	waif	frail	waning
frigid	shilling	sixpence	scowl	joviality
woeful	sumptuous	banquet	fragrant	sculpt

Discussion Questions

1. What did Thomas think of the sculpted candles the old man made?
2. What did Thomas say he needed?
3. Who was the first shadow to emerge? Who did Thomas think it was and what did he give her?
4. Who was the second form laying in the gutter? Who did Thomas think it was and what did he do for him?
5. What did Thomas suspect was strange?
6. What did Thomas do when he encountered the third person?
7. Was the town as empty as Thomas had told the old man it was?
8. What was the candle's purpose? What did it help Thomas do?
9. At story's end, did Thomas still think the old candle maker was foolish?
10. What did Thomas do when he realized the truth in the old man's words?
11. Who are the other "members of our family"?

12. What does the illumination of Christmas help us to see?
13. Thought he returned home penniless and poorer than he began, how did the Christmas candle makes Thomas richer?

Copywork

> You are costly, but of great worth.
> —words of the chandler in *The Christmas Candle*

> If we will see things as they truly are, we will find that all, from great to small, belong to one family. And this truth, known from the beginning of time, is perhaps seen best in the joyous illumination of Christmas.
> —the ending of *The Christmas Candle*

Parent's Help Page
(*The Christmas Candle*)

Observation
1. With your child imagine the ways Thomas was able to help the third person he returned to.

2. Review the corporal works of mercy with your child and discuss how you can address each work this holiday season: feed the hungry, give drink to the thirsty, clothe the naked, visit the imprisoned, shelter the homeless, visit the sick, bury the dead.

Discussion Answers
1. Thomas thought the sculpted candles were foolish.
2. Thomas said he needed a candle for illumination.
3. The first shadow was a beggar woman. Thomas thought she was his mother and gave her his cloak.
4. The second form was a man. Thomas thought he was his brother and found him a place to stay until he could return for him.
5. Thomas suspected the light from the candle was strange.
6. When Thomas encountered the third person he pulled the lantern away and left her.
7. No, the town was not as empty as Thomas thought it was.
8. The candle's purpose was to dispel the darkness and illuminate the world around Thomas. It helped him to see the poor, needy souls he would have otherwise overlooked.
9. Thomas realized the old man was very wise.
10. When Thomas realized what the old man had told him, he went out to check on the other "members of our family."
11. The other "members of our family" are the people we encounter everyday. They are our brothers and sisters in Christ.

12. The illumination of Christmas helps us to see those around us who need our care, our love, and our help.
13. The Christmas Candle opened Thomas' eyes to those around him and made him richer in spirit, charity, and generosity.

Enrichment Activity

1. Read 1 Corinthians 12:14-20, 24-26 (below) with your child and discuss how this Scripture verse relates to *The Christmas Candle:*

> For the body does not consist of one member but of many. If the foot should say, "Because I am not a hand, I do not belong in the body," that would not make it any less a part of the body. And if the ear should say, "Because I am not an eye, I do not belong to the body," that would not make it any less a part of the body. If the whole body were an eye, where would be the hearing? If the whole body were any ear, where would be the sense of smell? But as it is, God arranged the organs in the body, each one of them, as he chose. If all were a single organ, where would the body be (1 Cor. 12:14-20).

> But God has so adjusted the body, giving the greater honor to the inferior part, that there maybe no discord in the body, but that the members may have the same care for one another. If one member suffers, all suffer together; if one member is honored, all rejoice together (1 Cor. 12:24-26).

2. Purchase a wide white candle and glitter glue pens. Let your child decorate the candle and on it write the name "Jesus". Older children might be able to write "Jesus: Light of the World" on theirs. Many people switch from the purple and rose candles of Advent to a white candle on Christmas Eve or Christmas morning. You can use the candles that your children decorate for this purpose.

Christmas Candles

In the evening, in the windows,
red and white the candles glow,
so the Christ Child, if He passes,
will be guided through the snow.
No one knows what route He travels.
no one knows when He is nigh,
but each house that shows a candle
will be blessed if He goes by.
—Aileen Fisher

The Shoemaker's Dream
by Masahiro Kasuya/ Illustrated by Mildred Schell
Published by Judson Press, 1980.

Vocabulary

naughty   quarrel   ragged   shiver

Discussion Questions
1. What did Martin do for a living?
2. What does Jesus tell Martin in his dream?
3. Name each visitor that Martin had and tell what he did for the visitors.
4. Did Jesus visit the shoemaker that day? How?

Copywork

Your good tea has warmed my old bones.
Your good talk has warmed my heart.
                —the old man to Martin in *The Shoemaker's Dream*

I tell you, whenever you did this for one of the least important
of these brothers of mine, you did it for me.
                —from Matthew 25:40, quoted in *The Shoemaker's Dream*

Parent's Help Page
(*The Shoemaker's Dream*)

Observation

After reading the third page where Martin goes through his evening routine, see if your child can narrate his routine from memory:

- Cleaned the workbench
- Put away his tools
- Cooked his supper and ate it
- Washed the dishes
- Lit his lamp
- Read his Bible

Discussion Answers

1. Martin was a shoemaker.
2. Jesus told Martin that he would come to visit him.
3. The first visitor was an old man in a thin coat. Martin fed him and gave him a cup of tea. The second visitor was a mother and her baby. Martin brought them inside, warmed them, and gave the mother a warm jacket. The third visitors were a lady and a boy. Martin bid the lady to let the little boy go and remember "Jesus who loves little children…". He had the boy apologize to the lady for stealing her apple and settled their quarrel.
4. Yes. He was in the old man, the mother and her baby, and the lady and the boy.

Leo Tolstoy 1863

Enrichment Activity

1. Study and learn the Corporal Works of Mercy. Have your child write each work on an index card, and then find a picture from a magazine depicting someone offering a helping hand or kind act during the Christmas season. Have him cut out the picture and glue it on the opposite side of the appropriate index card. Trace a Christmas tree on a large green poster board, cut it out, and tape the cards on your tree to remind you to do for others this Christmas season.

2. Decide which activities you and your child could do this Christmas season:

   - Feed the hungry—visit a soup kitchen/ bring groceries to a needy family/ donate food to a care center or your church's pantry for the poor.
   - Give drink to the thirsty—same as above.
   - Clothe the naked—go through your clothes and see what can be donated to a care center/ purchase a toy to give to a shelter for a needy child.
   - Visit the imprisoned, shelter the homeless, visit the sick—these three can all be observed by visiting a nursing home, an elderly shut-in, or someone you know who is lonely this Christmas season.
   - Bury the dead—pray without ceasing.

3. Another book you and your child might want to read is *The Candle in the Window* by Grace Johnson and Mark Elliot.

4. Read *Shoemaker Martin* illustrated by Bernadette Watts, which is the same story as the *The Shoemaker's Dream*, but depicted by a different artist. Compare the two books and discuss each artist's style. Discuss how the artist creates a mood with color and style. Let the child say which one he/she likes best and explain why.

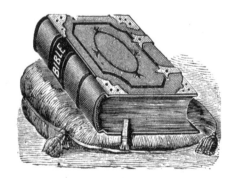

Why the Chimes Rang
by Raymond MacDonald Alden
Published by Guild Press of Indiana, Inc., 1994.

Vocabulary

shutter	organ	chime	archways	cast
rouse	chapel	procession	organist	aisle

Discussion Questions
1. What was the strangest thing about the old church?
2. What did people say the bells sounded like?
3. Who or what did people say rang the bells?
4. The legend of the Christmas bells said they only rang when a person did what?
5. Who did the brothers come upon on their way to the great church?
6. Who did the woman look like? Who is the Madonna?
7. What would happen to the woman if one of the boys did not stay with her while the other went for help?
8. What did Pedro give his little brother to give as an offering at the festival?
9. What was Pedro giving up by staying with the poor woman?
10. What did men bring to the altar in hopes of making the bells ring?
11. What did everyone think would surely make the bells ring? Did it?
12. What really made the bells chime?

13. Why was Pedro's little piece of silver the greatest gift to the Christ-child?
14. Do you think Pedro heard the Christmas bells ring over the snowy drifts on the plain?

Copywork

> "Nobody can guess, Little Brother, all the fine things there are to see
> and hear; and I have even heard it said that the Christ-child sometimes
> comes down to bless the service. What if we could see Him?"
>
> —Pedro to Little Brother in *Why the Chimes Rang*

Parent's Help Page
(*Why the Chimes Rang*)

Observation

Carefully observe the page borders throughout the book and discuss their significance as you read the page.

Discussion Answers

1. The strangest thing about the old church was the chime of bells.
2. People said the bells sounded like angels in the sky and like strange winds singing through trees.
3. People said the wind rang the bells. Others said the angels rang them.
4. The Christmas bells only rang when the "greatest and best offering was laid on the altar" for the Christ-child.
5. The brothers came upon a poor woman who was too sick and tired to seek shelter.
6. The woman resembled the Madonna in the chapel window. The Madonna is the Blessed Mother Mary.
7. The woman would freeze to death without their help.
8. Pedro gave his brother a little piece of silver to lie on the altar as his offering to the Christ-child.
9. By staying with the woman, Pedro was giving up the music and splendor and warmth and wonder of the festival in the beautiful old church on Christmas night.
10. Men gave jewels, baskets of gold, a book, and a crown.
11. They thought the king's crown would surely make the bells ring. No, it did not.
12. Pedro's little piece of silver had made the bells chime.
13. Pedro's gift made the bells chime because he had given up much more than anyone else by staying alone with the poor woman in the dark and cold while everyone else enjoyed the music and splendor of the Christmas festivities.
14. Listen carefully to your child's reply and ask him the reason why he thinks this.

Enrichment Activities

1. Use a bell cookie cutter and make bell shaped sugar cookies. (See the recipe in the Recipe Appendix.)
2. Using the same bell cookie cutter as a pattern, or a larger bell template, trace a set of bells on a piece of art paper. Have the child write or draw a gift that he could give to the child Jesus that might make the bells chime. Each child can make as many bells as he wants. Cut them out and then perhaps hang them around the manger scene or create a special poster on which to hang them.
3. *A Gift for the Christ Child* by Linda Schlafer and *The Polar Express* by Chris Van Allsburg (both about believing and having the faith of a child) are appropriate joint readings.

Song

Why do the bells of Christmas ring?
Why do little children sing?

Once a lovely shining star,
Seen by shepherds from afar,
Gently moved until its light
Made a manger's cradle bright.

There a darling baby lay,
Pillowed soft upon the hay;
And its mother sung and smiled:
"This is Christ, the holy Child!"

Therefore bells for Christmas ring,
Therefore little children sing.

—EUGENE FIELD

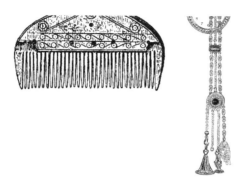

The Gift of the Magi
by O. Henry
(Various illustrated versions)

Vocabulary

bargain	shabby	cascade	platinum	elegant	trance
ecstatic	tortoise	tresses	reflection	prompt	hysterical
possession	ardent	lamely	magi	peculiar	yearn

Discussion Questions

1. How much money did Della have?
2. Why did she cry?
3. Why do you think the author makes it a point to stress how little money Della had?
4. What were the "two possessions…in which they both took great pride"?
5. What does Della do to get the money for Jim's present?
6. Why did Jim look at her so strangely when he got home?
7. What gift did Jim buy Della?
8. How did he get the money to buy the combs?
9. What makes this story ironic?
10. What thing did this couple value and love more than the watch and hair?
11. Who were the Magi and why is this story called "The Gift of the Magi"?

Copywork

Maybe the hairs on my head were numbered," she went on with a sudden serious sweetness, "but nobody could ever count my love for you.
> —words of Della to Jim in *The Gift of the Magi*

But in a last word to the wise of these days, let it be said that of all who give gifts, these two were the wisest, for theirs were the gifts of love.
> —*The Gift of the Magi* by O. Henry

Parent's Help Page
(The Gift of the Magi)

Observation

1. The author writes: "She stood by the window and looked out dully at a gray cat walking a gray fence in a gray backyard." What does this sentence tell you about how the day matches Della's mood?
2. Looking at the illustrations in Jody Wheeler, Lisbeth Zwerger, and Michael Dooling versions, one can tell the story takes place in the early part of the 20th century? What clues in the story show you this? (the style of clothing, the cost of living)
3. Keep list of clues found in story showing the couple's poor state:

   - Della did not have enough money for a Christmas gift
   - She had saved pennies for months to buy Jim's gift
   - The furnishing were scarce and the couch was shabby
   - The red carpet was worn
   - Della's jacket and hat were old

Discussion Answers

1. Della had $1.87.
2. She cried because the next day would be Christmas and she didn't have enough money.
3. The author makes a point of stressing the amount of money to show how poor they are and how precious the saving of her pennies is.
4. The two great possessions were Jim's gold watch and Della's long hair.
5. Della cuts her hair.
6. It was because of the gift he had bought for her.
7. He had bought her combs for her hair.
8. Jim sold his grandfather's watch to buy the combs.
9. The story is ironic because, in buying for each other what they thought would be the perfect gift, they each sacrificed the thing they valued the most and could not use the gift given to them.
10. This couple valued their love for one other more than the items they had sold.
11. The Magi were the three wise men who brought gifts to the baby Jesus. It is called "The Gift of the Magi" because, like this couple, the magi were wise and brought Christ gifts of love. In the words of O. Henry: "…let it be said that of all who give gifts, these two were the wisest, for theirs were the gifts of love."

Enrichment Activity

1. Jim's salary is $20.00 a week. The rent on the apartment is $8.00 a week. Give your child a math lesson in living. What does rent cost today? How much does your family have budgeted each week? Show your child the difference in the cost of living from when this story was written to today's cost of living.

2. What similes can your child find in this story?

- "So now Della's beautiful hair fell about her, rippling and shining like a cascade of brown waters.
- And then Della leaped up like a little burned cat and cried.

And the Grinch, with his Grinch-feet ice cold in the snow,
stood puzzling and puzzling, how could it be so?
It came without ribbons. It came without tags.
It came without packages, boxes or bags.
And he puzzled and puzzled 'till his puzzler was sore.
Then the Grinch thought of something he hadn't before.
What if Christmas, he thought, doesn't come from a store.
What if Christmas, perhaps, means a little bit more.

—From *The Grinch who Stole Christmas*
by Dr. Seuss

Instead of being a time of unusual behavior, Christmas is perhaps the only time in the year when people can obey their natural impulses and express their true sentiments without feeling self-conscious and, perhaps, foolish. Christmas, in short, is about the only chance a man has to be himself.

—Francis C. Farl, source unknown

The First Christmas Stocking

Written by Elizabeth Winthrop/ Illustrated by Bagram Ibatoulline

Published by Delacorte Press, 2006. Jacket Cover from *The First Christmas Stocking*
used by permission of Random House Children's Books,
a division of Random House, Inc.

Vocabulary

dainty	eternal	skeins	lull	consolation	snatch
skitter	pouch	drafty	kindling	sputter	hearth

Discussion Questions

1. What jobs do Claire's parents do?
2. What double meaning do you think the author intends by: "Because the sun rarely found its way to their door…"
3. How do we know the family is poor?
4. What does Claire's mom teach her to do?
5. What special things does the family do on Christmas Day?
6. What is Claire's only consolation after her mother died?
7. What is Claire's wish for her father after she gets the stocking order from the rich lady?
8. What does Claire knit into her stockings?

9. Why do you think Claire gives the socks to the boy she meets on the street?
10. What happened when the stockings are put on the boy's feet, hands, and head?
11. What does she sacrifice in giving these stockings to the boy?
12. How does Claire feel about the little ragged boy getting the stockings versus the rich children on the hill?
13. What Christmas miracle does Claire and her father experience?
14. Why are people drawn to Claire's home?

Copywork

Dream your dreams and knit them into the wool.
—words of Claire's mother in *The First Christmas Stocking*

Your mother is knit into you, just as your dreams are knit into the wool.
—words of Claire's father in *The First Christmas Stocking*

Parent's Help Page
(*The First Christmas Stocking*)

Observation
1. Observing what the little boy feels when the stockings are put on his feet, hands, and head, list the dreams that Claire dreamed as she knitted her stockings:
   - A warm kitchen hearth
   - A puddle of hot summer mud
   - Strong grasp of father
   - Tight circle of mother's fingers
   - Music of bells

2. Does your child notice what is tied around the candles and bundle of kindling that Claire pulls from her stocking? (a scrap of green scarf) Where have you seen this in the book? (wrapped around the little ragged boy's neck)

Discussion Answers
1. Claire's father is a coal miner and her mother is a knitter.
2. This could mean that the family did not often have good luck and were often burdened by the hardships in life.
3. We know the family is poor because of their frugal use of candles and firewood and because the mother knits for the rich people of the town.
4. Claire's mom teaches her to knit.
5. The mother makes currant cakes and spiced cider. Claire's toes are warm and there is a lot of light in the home.
6. Claire's only consolation is to knit while rocking in her mother's rocking chair.

7. Claire's wish is to make Christmas just the way Mother had always made it.
8. Claire knits her dreams into her stockings.
9. Claire gives him all but one of the stockings because she knows how it feels to not feel your feet because of the cold.
10. The boy feels the dreams that Claire knit into the stockings.
11. She sacrifices the spiced cider, the cakes, her father's pouch of tobacco, and the light and warmth of the Christmas fire.
12. Claire feels that the children at the top of the hill wouldn't appreciate her stockings the way the little boy does because they already have so much.
13. The candle wax never drips and their fire never dies down. Claire receives lots of orders for her stockings.
14. People are drawn to Claire's little house because of the warmth and welcome they receive there.

Enrichment Activities

1. Cut out a large stocking made from construction paper or cardstock. On this stocking, draw or cut out from a magazine all your wishes and dreams. How are they the same or different from Claire's?

2. Cut out three smaller stockings and staple or glue sides and bottom to full sheet of paper, leaving top of stocking open. Label one stocking Jesus, one stocking Family, and another stocking Others. Every time your child thinks of something thoughtful or kind he can do for someone, have him write the deed on a slip of paper and drop it inside the appropriate stocking.

3. Consider the following quote in light of the story.

> For thou didst form my inward parts,
> Thou didst knit me together in my mother's womb.
> —Psalms 139:13

Let you child think long on this quote and idea of knitting your dreams into what you knit. What has God knit into us? Think about Jesus being formed in Mary's womb.

4. Make spiced cider and currant cakes.

Currant Cake Recipe
1 cup butter, softened
$1\frac{1}{2}$ cups sugar
1 t. salt
2 large eggs
1 10-oz box (about $1\frac{3}{4}$ cups) currants (raisins can be used as a substitute)
$4\frac{1}{2}$ cups all-purpose flour
2 t. baking powder

2 t. baking soda

$1\frac{1}{2}$ cups buttermilk

Grease 2 $8\frac{1}{2}$ X $4\frac{1}{2}$ loaf pans. Line the bottom with parchment paper. (This is not absolutely necessary, but will help the loaves brown better on the bottom and make it much easier to get the loaves out of the pans. You can butter the top of the parchment very lightly.)

Cream together the butter, sugar, and salt. Add the eggs, one at a time, beating well after each addition until mixture is smooth and fluffy. Toss the currants in about 2 T of the measured flour. Stir the baking powder and the baking soda into the remaining flour. Stir half the flour into the egg butter mixture. Then stir in the buttermilk. Stir in the remaining flour, then stir vigorously or beat on lowest speed about minute until well blended. Stir in the currants. Scrape it into the prepared pans and bake at 350° for 1.25 hours, until a deep golden color. A knife or toothpick inserted should come out clean. Cook in pans on a rack. Unmold and peel away parchment paper. Slice in thick chunks (it will be crumbly). Try toasting the pieces and spreading with butter.

Spiced Cider

    1 gallon Cider

    4 small cinnamon sticks

    20 whole cloves

    $\frac{1}{2}$ t. nutmeg (optional)

Blend cider, cinnamon, cloves, and nutmeg (if desired) in a crock pot. Heat on high until the cider is hot, then turn to low and leave until serving time. You can heat this on a stove in a heavy saucepan on a very temperature as well. Serve it with a cinnamon stick in each mug, but be careful to sieve out the cloves before drinking.

The Bears' Christmas Surprise
Written by Bruno Hachler/ Illustrated by Angela Kehlenbeck
Published by North-South Books, 2000.

Vocabulary

neglect   balcony   squiggly   mute

Discussion Questions
1. Why was the bear's fur dull and shaggy?
2. Why did he still have a glow in his eyes?
3. Where do you think all the teddy bears were going?
4. What did the bears do in the houses?
5. What happened Christmas morning: what do the children do? What do the parents do?
6. What does the note (found here in the copywork section) mean?
7. Where had the bears taken the gifts?
8. Your child might not like the idea of not getting a Christmas gift on Christmas morning and giving it to someone else. Discuss this with him. What is the true meaning of this story?
9. The bear at the story's end is no longer played with. Why does he look shabbier than before? Does he find joy in what he does? How do you know this?

101

Copywork

> This package is as empty as my arms.
> My heart remembers when you ran to me with joy.
> I am longing for a cheerful visit.
> Do you remember me? I often think of you.
> —The *Bears' Christmas Surprise*

Parent's Help Page
(*The Bears' Christmas Surprise*)

Discussion Answers

1. The bear's fur was dull and shaggy from "hours of play and then neglect".
2. He remembered the first time a child held him.
3. Listen to your child's answer. Let him explore his imagination.
4. They unwrapped gifts and left squiggly notes inside then took the gifts to other houses.
5. Listen as your child explains what happened when the children opened their gifts and found nothing but a note inside.
6. The note left by the bears was a reminder to the people to remember all the lonely people in the city.
7. The bears had taken the gifts to the lonely people in the city.
8. The true meaning in this story is that during Christmas more than any other season we need to practice the virtues of giving and caring for our fellowman. Christmas shouldn't be just about us. We should open our arms and our hearts to others who have less or are lonely.
9. The bear looks shabbier because he gives of himself to others. Yes, he finds joy in this. You can tell this from the glimmer in his eyes.

Enrichment Activities

1. Who do you know who is lonely? Do you know a child who will not have a good Christmas this year? What can you do to make Christmas better for other people?

2. Discuss with your child something your family can do to help someone less fortunate:
   * Adopt a family
   * Visit a nursing home
   * Buy a gift for a needy child, something as expensive as a new bike or as priceless as a teddy bear
   * Visit the pediatric ward in a hospital
   * Serve at a soup kitchen
   * Donate food/clothes/toys to a charity center
   * Think of ideas particular to your community.

A Small Miracle
by Peter Collington
Published by Alfred A. Knopf, 1997.

A Small Miracle is illustrated in frames without the use of a single word. There is a story there, however, "written" through the pictures. The best way to appreciate such a book is to study each frame and discover the story within the artwork.

Briefly, for the parent, this story is about teaching the Golden Rule to your children: "Do unto others as you would have them do to you."

For each page in *A Small Miracle*, there is a description in this guide of what takes place. This will aid the parent reader in pointing out things to the child and serve as a guide sheet. Let your child go through the pages once or twice just looking at the pictures and thinking about them. Let him ask questions and wonder out loud about them. Then tell him he is going to tell the story that the pictures portray. Keep a sheet of paper with you as you go through the book and write what the child says as he tells the story. Discuss each page with him as needed.

Page 1:
A poor elderly woman wakes to a freezing dawn. Her dwellings are sparse. You can tell she's poor from the hole in the floor and the bare furnishings. The frosted windowpanes and blanket around her thin shoulders shivers the season and blankets the chill to the reader.

Page 2:
She has nothing to eat and no wood to burn. Her cash box is empty.

Page 3-5:
She must go out and play her music in hopes of an offering with which to buy some food.

Page 6-9:
She passes by the church where the Nativity Crèche is being set-up and enters the town where Christmas vibrates in the air. Ask your child which symbols of Christmas he sees. She begins to play her accordion in hopes of receiving some money to buy something to eat and perhaps some wood for fire.

Page 10:
When no one gives her any donation, she must sell her beloved accordion, the only thing of value she owns.

Page 11-13:
But her money box is stolen by a thief. She crosses paths with the thief once again as he leaves the church with the money pail for the poor. She is able to get the pail away from him and takes refuge in the church.

Page 14-15:
She discovers the thief has vandalized the church and the Christmas crèche. She devotes herself to rearranging the beloved nativity figures into their rightful places.

Page 16-17:
Hungry, worn, old, and spent, she sets out for home but soon collapses in the snow before reaching her gypsy wagon.

Page 18-20:
But Christmas is a time for miracles.

On the horizon appear the nativity figures of Mary, Joseph, three kings, and a shepherd boy who assist the old woman, get her to the safety of her home, and care for her.

Page 21-22:
While Mary, in quiet servitude, nurses the old woman at her bedside, the three kings travel to the pawn shop where the old woman sold her beloved accordion.

Page 23:
The three kings sell their valuable treasurers to the shopkeeper and buy back the old woman's treasured accordion.

Page 24-25:
With the rest of the money, the three kings go to the store and pick up groceries which they carry to her wagon. We see that Joseph has cut some firewood for her and a warm fire hugs the stove inside.

Page 26-27:
These two pages are the focal point of the whole book. They tie together all the pages on the single, shiny thread of tinsel that is Christmas.

The three kings are busy cooking the food they bought, St. Joseph repairs the hole in the floor, and the shepherd boy decorates the Christmas tree that St. Joseph cut in the woods.

As Joseph takes the infant Jesus from Mary so that she might climb down from her vigilant spot next to the old woman, we are reminded of the reason for the season.

St. Joseph's out-stretched hands to the Christ Child reminds us that all we have comes from Him and that it is through one others' hands that we give and that we receive.

Page 28-29:
The old woman awakes and is amazed. The candles upon the tree shine upon the bounty before her. A hot meal awaits her. She peeks out the door but sees no one. In the large center frame, you can point out to your child the red robe of one of the kings and Mary's blue robe as they walk back towards the horizon.

Page 30:
As the warmth of Christmas surrounds her, the old woman sings its praises. A lovely single star shines over her small gypsy wagon.

Discussion
1. Why did the woman take the time to reset all the nativity figures?
2. Does she have the spirit of Christmas? Explain
3. Why did the Nativity figures help the old woman?

Enrichment Activity
1. Your child will know that crèche figures cannot really come to life but explain to him about how Christmas is a time for miracles (for example, the birth of Christ was a miracle) and how we, through our own hands, can makes miracles come true for others. Try to think of something your child can do secretly for someone else during this season.
2. Encourage your child to create a story without words. Divide a sheet of paper into 4 boxes and illustrate the story in a sequence of pictures. Add extra page if needed. This could be a gift that the child makes for someone special, like an elderly relative, or the postman, or the parish priest.
3. Using a set of child friendly nativity figures, have your child reenact the story.

A Reflection on Santa Claus

By Cay Gibson

In 1897, a little girl wrote the intriguing question "Is There a Santa Claus?" to a local newspaper. The lead editorial writer, Francis P. Church, then penned that famous reply: "Yes, Virginia, there is a Santa Claus." Although these words were written over 100 years ago, the message has not lost its luster. This Christmas I got to see the wisdom of these words through the eyes of an 80-year-old grandfather who is confined to a wheelchair and living in the inescapable world of Alzheimer's Disease.

We visited PawPaw (our nickname for Grandpa) the other night with two gifts: a stuffed dog with bulging comical eyeballs and a large white snowman stuffed with chocolate chip cookies. PawPaw always loved dogs, anything considered funny, and—most of all—sweet treats.

My husband fed PawPaw a cup of strawberry yogurt and teased him about his unkempt hair. He then questioned him about the sore on his arm, trying to open a window into his elderly father's mind.

"Dad, what's Gerald been up to?" No response.

"Have you seen Rusty lately? What about Don?" Silence.

"Rusty said Yogi came to visit you. Remember Yogi? You worked with him for years."

"Yogi Bear! Yogi Bear!" our four-year-old shouted, as she skipped around PawPaw's wheelchair, happily clacking the toes and heels of her church shoes on the floor.

"What about Frenchie-girl here?" We always brought the family dog with us to the nursing home. The nursing staff encouraged us doing so and PawPaw always remembered Frenchie, even after he had forgotten who we were.

"Remember Frenchie chasing those squirrels in your yard?" my husband probed for a memory his dad would recall. PawPaw just stared at his youngest son.

"Hey, Dad, guess who went to the Superdome this year and played for the state championship?" PawPaw simple blinked and opened his mouth for another bite of yogurt.

"The Tors football team did. Didn't you play for the Sulphur Tors? Didn't you take the Tors to the state championship the year you graduated?" The veil over PawPaw's eyes thickened. The window remained shut.

"Do you remember playing with Jimmie Barkate? Bill Lawton? Glenn Brousssard?"

We had hoped that the mind that couldn't remember his sons or the family sitting on the couch in front of him would remember childhood playmates. But his mind remained closed.

Still, my husband searched the past, hoping his dad would meet him in some distant memory. "What about Aunt Joann? Millie? Have you heard from them?" No response. Not even mention of childhood siblings lifted the curtain of that veiled window.

My husband scraped the edges of the yogurt container and we sat in silence. Paw Paw's mind had drifted to the point where his only pleasure was the arm rubs and back massages his son gave him. Like a baby bird, he was totally dependant on others. He resided in a nest that those around had made for him and he automatically opened his mouth to food as his only lifeline. The only connection this Navy veteran made with those around him was in singing World War II songs with his daughter-in-law and in reciting the Our Father with anyone who took the time to stop and say it with him.

Suddenly, eyeing the Christmas tree lights blinking nearby, and the felt Santa hanging on a nearby door, my husband cheerfully said, "Dad, guess who's fixing to come to town next week?" PawPaw's eyes blinked as his toothless gums chewed relentlessly at the pieces of fruit in his mouth. No response.

"Santa! Santa's coming!" my husband told him joyfully as our four-year-old skipped excitedly around PawPaw singing, "Santa! Santa!"

And, suddenly, from the inner recesses of a mind lost to disease, PawPaw laughed. It was a deep, from-the-gut belly chuckle. "No kiddin'," he laughed with full recognition. The curtain was lifted. The window opened a crack.

"He sure is," his youngest son assured him, as though he truly believed it himself. "And he's bringing you a present!"

My husband was delighted to see even a hint of the father he remembered. He took joy that the man who had been his childhood Santa Claus had made a brief appearance in front of the Christmas tree on a December night. The excitement in both their eyes was that unmistakable look often found on Christmas morning—in the eyes of fathers and sons alike.

During the rest of our visit, anytime we mentioned Santa, PawPaw's eyes lit up, his face cleared, and he laughed with childhood delight. His little granddaughters shared the laughter and excitement with him. Finally here was a moment they could enjoy together.

As we got up to leave, we took turns hugging and kissing PawPaw. As I bent down to kiss his check, I took the opportunity to remind him, "Be a good boy, PawPaw. Remember, Santa is coming."

No response. The window had closed.

Still, as I looked around that nursing home living area, I realized that Francis P. Church was right. There was a Santa. There could be no doubt. Santa Claus was found in the twinkling lights and greenery of the Christmas tree, in the nursing home staff who had fed my father-in-law his dinner that night, in the gifts that family had brought their loved ones, in the school choirs that would visit and sing for the residents, and in the little nativity setting on the mantelpiece. In the open arms of the Christ child smiling from the confines of his humble, straw-scented manger, I saw that He welcomed everyone; those who come to Him full of life and those who are brought to Him filled with childlike faith.

> He exists as certainly as love and generosity and devotion exist,
> and you know that they abound and give to your life its highest beauty
> and joy. Alas! How dreary would be the world if there were no Santa
> Claus! It would be as dreary as if there were no Virginias. There would
> be no childlike faith then, no poetry, no romance to make tolerable this
> existence. We should have no enjoyment, except in sense and sight. The
> external light with which childhood fills the world would be
> extinguished.
>
> —by Francis P. Church
> *The New York Sun*, 1897

Santa lives in the hearts and minds of little children just as he takes up residence in the minds of old men and women. He might not be *real,* but he is part of the poetry, the romance, the art, and the beauty that makes up Christmas. He certainly represents the faith of Christmas day: the faith we have in Our Savior, in our caretakers, in our loved ones, in our parents, and in all those who play the role of Santa in our lives.

In my opinion this integration of Santa with the sacred day of Christmas is most beautifully exemplified in the image of Santa Claus kneeling in homage before the Christ child in the manger. With this as your centerpiece at Christmastime, no explanation to the children in your home is needed. They will grow up with that childish faith that will sustain them for life. They will see that Jesus openly welcomes and embraces their childish faith. If you believe in poetry and romance and art and believe that these things make life more beautiful and worth living, then you cannot help but imagine Santa kneeling next to that cradle. Santa and the Christ Child: What a joyful "reality." What a beautiful Christmas duet! What a lovely work of art.

A Real Santa Claus

Santa Claus, I hang for you,
By the mantel, stockings two:
One for me and one to go
To another boy I know.

There's a chimney in the town
You have never traveled down.
Should you chance to enter there
You would find a room all bare:
Not a stocking could you spy,
Matters not how you might try;
And the shoes, you'd find are such
As no boy would care for much.
In a broken bed you'd see
Some one just about like me,
Dreaming of the pretty toys
Which you bring to the other boys,
And to him a Christmas seems
Merry only in his dreams.

All he dreams then, Santa Claus,
Stuff the stockings with, because
When it's filled up to the brim
I'll be Santa Claus to him!
                    —Frank Dempster Sherman

Santa's Favorite Story
Written by Hisako Aoki/ Illustrated by Ivan Gantschev
Published by Aladdin, 1997.

Discussion Questions
1. What was the first animal to see Santa in the forest?
2. Why was Santa out hiking?
3. What is Santa's favorite story?
4. What was the first Christmas gift God gave to the world?
5. What is better than any present you can get for Christmas?
6. What message do you think the author wants the reader to understand through this story?

Copywork

> Love was the gift God gave to us on the first Christmas, and it still is, you know. And this love is far better than any presents I can ever deliver.
> —Santa to the animals in *Santa's Favorite Story*

> How silly we have been to think that Christmas is only about presents.
> —The fox to the other animals in *Santa's Favorite Story*

Parent's Help Page
(*Santa's Favorite Story*)

Discussion Answers
1. The first animal to see Santa in the forest was a fox.
2. Santa was hiking to get into shape for Christmas Eve.
3. Santa's favorite story is the birth of the Christ child.
4. God's first Christmas gift to the world was Love through the gift of His son.
5. The thing better than any present is the gift of God's love.
6. Listen carefully to your child. Make sure he understands that even Santa knows that Christ is the reason for the season.

Enrichment Activity
1. Find a picture of Santa Claus and a picture of the Infant Jesus. Fold a red or green cardstock in half and glue the picture of Santa Claus at the top of one side and the picture of the Infant Jesus at the top of the other side of the fold. Under the picture of Santa Claus, try to remember and write down all the gifts you have received in past Christmases. Under the picture of the Infant Jesus, write "The Gift of Love! This is God's Gift to Me!"

A Reflection on St. Nicholas

By Mary Ellen Barrett

"He came mommy, St Nicholas came," is the delighted cry heard on the morning of every Saint Nicholas Day in my home for the last few years. Having grown up with a Santa tradition, but not Saint Nicholas, I was delighted to read of this great Saint and incorporate his feast day into our Advent preparations.

While expecting my fourth child my husband was enrolled in our parish RCIA program and I was trying to incorporate as much of our Catholic heritage and culture into our daily lives as possible. I wanted to make our home as much a part of his preparation to enter the Church as I could. So during one of the frequent library trips I made with my small children I pulled Ann Trompert's *Saint Nicholas* from the shelf and took it home to read to everybody. While growing up I knew that Santa was a legend grown out of the Saint Nicholas story but I was completely unaware of the immense effect that this great saint had on generations of Catholics. Trompert's book inspired me to find out more, and since then St. Nicholas Day has been a much anticipated part of our Advent preparation.

I discovered that all around the world Saint Nicholas Day is a joyful celebration and a large part of the Advent season. It is the primary gift giving day in many countries, leaving Christmas Day as a true holy day focused solely on the Christ child. Thousands of pilgrims flock to the shrine of *Noel Baba*, or Father Christmas, in Turkey every year to honor the saint whose humble and giving life is so much a part of their heritage.

When my family was younger I focused on telling stories, reading books, and coloring pictures of Saint Nicholas. Each year my young children would solemnly pick out their best (and biggest) pair of shoes to leave out for Saint Nicholas, and my husband and I would wait and listen in great anticipation for the little footsteps in the morning and to their reaction to the treats in their shoes. The most delightful treat, of course, being chocolate coins to represent the dowry money Saint Nicholas gave to three impoverished sisters in order that they might marry. Saint Nicholas also leaves holy cards depicting his image and chaplets for the boys and pins for the girls to wear to church in his honor. Breakfast may be *Speculaas* (spice cookies) and hot cocoa or, if I'm really on the ball, we follow the French tradition of *mannala*, brioche baked in the shape of a miter.

As the children have grown older and we have been blessed with more little ones, our Saint Nicholas Day has taken on another focus. This great Saint inherited a sizable fortune from his parents and he gave all of it away to the poor. He lived in a time when the early Christians were persecuted for their faith and he did what he could to ease their material suffering as well as minister to their souls. He was the Bishop of Myra and lived the Gospel he preached to those whose spiritual well being was under his auspices. Now I try to create an atmosphere of charitable giving around our Saint Nicholas Day celebrations. We make gift bags for the Franciscan Friars, little brown lunch sacks filled with shampoos, toothpaste, sewing kits, and other small toiletries that are welcome luxuries to these austere but joyful religious.

On the occasion of our twin babies' second Christmas we gathered all of their outgrown clothing and gear and made a large donation to our local life center. The children also contributed some of their Christmas money to include a monetary donation.

Since Saint Nicholas is Patron and Protector of children I thought this would be a wonderful way to commemorate his life, his love of Christ and the Child whose birth we so eagerly await.

Saint Nicholas Brioche

1 ¾ cup white flour
2 tsp Dried yeast
2 tsp sugar
1 cup Milk, tepid
1/3rd cup unsalted butter, at room temperature, softened and creamed
1 1/3 tsp Salt
1 egg , beaten
1 egg yolk + 1 tsp Water (for the egg wash)

Sprinkle the sugar and yeast into 1 cup of the milk in a bowl. Leave for 5 minutes and then stir to dissolve. Sieve the flour into a big bowl. Make a well and pour in the yeasted milk. With a wooden spoon, draw enough of the flour into the yeasted milk to form a soft paste. Cover with a tea towel and leave to "sponge" until frothy and risen, about 20 minutes.

Add the leftover milk, the beaten egg, salt and the creamed butter. Mix in the flour to form a soft dough. Turn the dough out onto a well-floured surface and knead until smooth and elastic for about 10 minutes. Put the dough into a buttered bowl and cover with a tea towel. Leave to rise until doubled in size, about 1 1/2 - 2 hours.

Knock back the dough and leave to rest for 10 minutes. Divide the dough into 10 equal pieces. Roll each piece into a thick sausage. Flatten out. Use a cookie cutter or finger shape into a miter. Place the miters on a baking sheet lined with baking paper and cover with a tea towel. Leave to rise doubled in size, about 30-40 minutes.

Preheat oven to 350°F. Brush the miters twice with the egg wash. Bake for about 20-25 minutes until golden and sounding hollow when tapped on the underside.

Speculaas (or Speculatius)—Dutch Spice Cookies
Contributed by Jennifer Miller

2 cups unsalted butter
2 cups brown sugar, firmly packed
½ cup sour cream
½ teaspoon baking soda
4 teaspoons cinnamon
½ teaspoon ground nutmeg
½ teaspoon ground cloves
4½ cups all-purpose flour, sifted
½ cup chopped nuts (pecans or walnuts)

113

Sift together flour, baking soda, cinnamon, nutmeg, and cloves. Set aside. Cream the butter and sugar. Add sour cream alternately with sifted dry ingredients. Stir in the nuts. Knead the dough into rolls. Wrap the rolls in wax paper and chill them in the refrigerator overnight. Roll the dough until it is very thin and then cut into shapes. Bake in moderate oven (375°) for 10 to 15 minutes.

Part of the dough can be cut into various shapes, such as birds, fish, or animals, using a knife or cookie cutters. Sometimes we ice these with white or pink icing, and decorate them with dried or candied fruits.

Recipe adapted by Jennifer Miller from Florence Berger, *Cooking for Christ*, copyright 1949, National Catholic Rural Life Conference. See http://www.catholicculture.org/liturgicalyear/recipes/view.cfm?id=169 for complete text.

Sean Fitzpatrick©2007 *Fenestrae Fidei*

For further Internet reading or references on St. Nicholas from the Internet, see the following websites (These are intended for parent/adult use.):

http://www.stnicholascenter.org/ St. Nicholas Center
http://www.wf-f.org/st.nicholas.html Women for Faith and Family, St. Nicholas
http://www.catholicculture.org/liturgicalyear/calendar/day.cfm?date=2006-12-06 Catholic Culture, St. Nicholas
http://www.domestic-church.com/CONTENT.DCC/19981101/SAINTS/nicholas.htm Domestic Church
http://maryellenb.typepad.com/o_night_divine/2006/11/saint_nicholas_.html St. Nicholas Part One
http://maryellenb.typepad.com/o_night_divine/2006/11/saint_nicholas__2.html St. Nicholas Part Two

Christmas Alphabet

A for the animals out in the stable.
B for the Babe in their manger for cradle.
C for the Carols so blithe and gay.
D for December, the twenty-fifth day.
E for the Eve when we're all so excited.
F for the Fire when the Yule Log is lighted.
G for the Goose which you all know is fat.
H is the Holly you stick in your hat.
I for the Ivy which clings to the wall.
J is for Jesus the cause of it all.
K for the Kindness begot by this feast.
L is the Light shining way in the East.
M for the Mistletoe. Beware where it hangs!
N is the Nowell the angels first sang.
O for the Oxen, the first to adore Him.
P for the Presents Wise Men laid before Him.
Q for the Queerness that this should have been,
  Near two thousand years before you were seen.
R for the Romps and the Raisins and Nuts.
S for the Stockings that Santa Claus stuffs.
T for the Toys on the Christmas Tree hanging.
U is for Us over the world ranging.
V for the Visitors welcomed so warmly.
W the Waits at your doors singing heartily!
X Y X bother me! All I can say,
Is this is the end of my Christmas lay.
So now to you all, wherever you be,
A merry merry Christmas, and many may you see!
                                    —Author Unknown

~ Advent Week Three ~

Family
Hanukkah

Sean Fitzpatrick

117

A Reflection on Family

By Dawn Hanigan

In all the year, what day is more joyous than Christmas? To a child, there simply is none.

For Christmas joy is *special*. It's a joy we carry in our hearts all year long—indeed, all *life* long. The fondest memories we have are often centered around this joyous holiday. Why? Because Christmas is spent with those we love best.

But Christmas is much more than just one day—it's a whole *season* of joys, big and small. There's so much to anticipate, and there will be so much to remember.

Consider Christmas Eve itself—a night with special dresses and shiny shoes, a quiet drive to church under starry skies; a night when children press their tiny noses against frosty windowpanes, tap their toes on polished floors, and smile their candy cane smiles. The air is thick with evergreen, ginger, and sweet anticipation.

Then one by one they arrive—grandmothers, grandfathers, aunts, uncles, and cousins; so many beautiful faces that light up the winter night, so many familiar voices that rise together in song. Young hearts drink in these joys and are filled to the brim with cherished memories.

The best memories are made in this season: the simple, close-knit gatherings, when our homes are peaceful and warm. Yet, for day and weeks before this grand celebration, we bake cookies and make a batch of Nana's special fudge. We sing hymns around the piano and bring home the perfect tree from the farm. We might linger after church to visit the crèche, and then light candles in prayer back at home. And so many afternoons are spent sharing special stories —the beloved books brought out only at Christmas. We curl up with mugs of cocoa as we share the stories that allow us to experience the wonder of Christmas through the eyes of others.

These are all just little things, but shared together, these little things become big in the heart of a child. They cherish the first snowflakes that fall, the first cup of hot cocoa, the bells in the air, the cards in the mail, the books strewn and read around the Christmas tree. All these moments that pass in a family's Christmas are moments that glow deep in our memory.

Time spent with family—whether it's just with Grandma and Grandpa, or with dozens of family members and dear friends—is time spent forming our memories and sharing our faith. It's the time our children will look on and fondly carry forward with them all the years of their lives.

Create space for those memories to grow. Gather your dear little ones around you this Christmas and share all the joys of the season. For the child who carries his family and faith in his heart is a very blessed child indeed. And what better place to honor the brightest and most beautiful of all Christmas joys—the birth of our Lord, and the beauty of His Holy Family—than right here in the midst of our own?

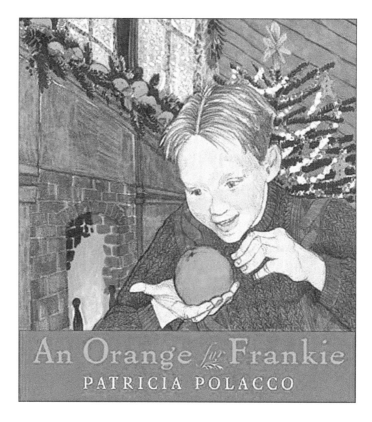

An Orange for Frankie
Written and illustrated by Patricia Polacco
Published by Philomel Books, Division of Penguin Young Readers Group, 2004.

Vocabulary

hurtle	chuff	hoecakes	crock	stoke	hobo
lye	bough	spectacles	wither	parlor	scold
muffler	fondant	scurry	tog	soapstone	burlap
dray	hillock	lament	fray	aroma	wedge

Discussion Questions

1. Who were the guests that arrived at the family's back door?
2. What was Frankie's job when the guests arrived?
3. What did Frankie give to Jump-Up Billy?
4. Where had Frankie's pa gone?
5. What did the family put on the mantle?
6. Why did Mr. Dunkle bring Pa home?
7. How was Frankie disobedient?
8. What happened to Frankie's orange?
9. Does Frankie do the right thing in confessing that he took the orange? Explain.
10. Why do the family members each give Frankie a part of their own oranges?

Copywork

> But you did a noble thing too, giving something that meant so much to you to someone who needed it. That is the true spirit of Christmas, my darlin'.
>
> Our family is like your orange, Frankie. Love holds us together like that there ribbon.
>
> —*An Orange for Frankie*

Parent's Help Page
(*An Orange for Frankie*)

Observation

1. See if your child remembers what the family in the story uses to decorate the tree: strings of berries and popcorn, dried flowers, and frosted cookies.

2. In the story, Frankie plays the part of "a perfect archangel". Ask your child if he sees the irony in this image (an angel who has just disobeyed his pa) and how this affects the way Frankie feels about himself.

Discussion Answers

1. The train engineer and hobos.
2. Frankie's job was to refill the hobos' cups with hot coffee.
3. Frankie gave Jump-Up Billy his best sweater.
4. Frankie's pa had gone to Lansing to get oranges for Christmas.
5. The family placed greens, apples, nuts, dried flowers, holly sprigs, and—the crowning glory—oranges.
6. Mr. Dunkle, the train engineer, brought Pa home. He was kind to Pa because of the kindness Ma showed him and the hobos when they passed through Locke Center.
7. Frankie took an orange off the mantle.
8. Frankie lost his orange.
9. Yes. You might discuss how difficult it is to admit when we've done something wrong.
10. The family each takes a wedge out of their own oranges and wraps the wedges in a ribbon for Frankie to show Frankie forgiveness and remind him that he is still part of the family.

Enrichment Activities

1. If you can find the out-of-print book *The Christmas Promise*, it is a good book to read in conjunction with this one.
2. Make the following recipe with your children.

Orange Snowballs
contributed by Dawn Hanigan

1 cup (or 2 sticks) unsalted butter
$\frac{1}{3}$ cup granulated sugar
$\frac{1}{2}$ teaspoon vanilla
$\frac{1}{2}$ teaspoon orange extract
2 cups flour

Topping:

1 cup powdered sugar
$\frac{1}{2}$ teaspoon orange Kool-aid ® unsweetened drink mix powder

Cream together the butter, sugar, vanilla, and orange extract. Add flour and mix until mixture is doughy. Roll into one-inch balls and place one-inch apart on an ungreased cookie sheet. Bake at 350°F for 15 minutes.

While cookies bake, mix together the powdered sugar and orange flavored drink mix. Roll warm cookies into this mixture and cool on a wire rack. Dust tops with extra powdered sugar using a sieve.

Makes 3 dozen tangy-sweet orange-shaped cookies that melt like snow in your mouth.

Silent Night
Written and Illustrated by Will Moses
Published by Puffin Books, 1997.

Vocabulary

commons	proprietor	toboggans	headwaters	frolic
gangly	gorge	satchel	lurch	rousted

Discussion Questions
1. Why was today no ordinary day for Tom Henry and Andy?
2. Who was Pa going to get at the station?
3. Why do you suppose Tom Henry called Grandma Stokes "General Grant"?
4. Describe how Grandma fit this name when she arrived at the house.
5. What did the family do while they waited?
6. What was the Christmas surprise?
7. What did Andy give his baby sister?

Copywork
Have your child copy neatly the chapter headings as you read through the book. By the end, your child will have written the first stanza to the Christmas carol "Silent Night."

Silent night, holy night!
All is calm, all is bright,
Round yon virgin mother and child!
Holy infant, so tender and mild,
Sleep in heavenly peace,
Sleep in heavenly peace.

Parent's Help Page
(*Silent Night*)

Observation

1. After reading the first two pages, have your child narrate (from memory) what the people were busy doing around town and see if he can point out the characters and locations in the picture.
2. Keep a list of the clues that something special was happening this night:
   - The boys did not play around on the ice but went straight home.
   - Their father said, "It's a holy-night, boys. You'll want to remember this night."
   - Pa did not stop the sleigh for the boys to skate as he normally did.
   - When Pa said, "It's a miracle." Andy knew he was taking about more than the glass star.

Discussion Answers

1. Something special was happening at their house and they were bringing home a Christmas tree.
2. Pa was going to pick-up Grandma Stokes at the train station.
3. Answers will vary. If the child knows what a general does, he might predict that Grandma Stokes was a kind of person who could give orders and make things happen.
4. Once in the house, Grandma Stokes began to issue orders to everyone.
5. While they waited the family trimmed the Christmas tree.
6. The Christmas surprise was a Christmas baby born that night.
7. Andy gave his baby sister his precious skates and a promise to "teach you to skate just like me and Tom Henry."

Enrichment Activities

1. Learn and practice the song "Silent Night." It's especially moving to sing it softly on Christmas Eve with just candles lit around the manger scene.
2. Have your child use the copy work to make a card for someone. He can print the words to the song on one side and illustrate a nativity scene on the other side.

The Christmas Promise
Written by Susan Bartoletti / Illustrated by David Christiana
Published by The Blue Sky Press, Imprint of Scholastic, Inc., 2001. (Out-of-Print)

Vocabulary

redball   hobo   kindle   freight   switchman   shanty

Discussion Questions
1. What time of year does the story begin?
2. What do you think the railroad bull's job was and why did the little girl and her father sneak into a boxcar?
3. Was this an honest thing to do?
4. What was the little girl's father searching for?
5. What were some of the dangers of a hobo's life?
6. How did hobos protect themselves from the cold?
7. Where did they sleep when it became too cold?
8. How did they keep other hobos from stealing their shoes?
9. What did the mission lady teach the little girl to do?
10. What did the little girl pray for?
11. What symbol did the father sign on his daughter's hand twice in this story and what did it mean?
12. What sign was scratched on the curb in front of twenty-three Weatherby Lane?
13. Were the little girl's prayer for "someplace good" answered? Was she happy?
14. What promise did her Poppa make to her?
15. Was the lady kind and was twenty-three Weatherby Lane "someplace good"? How can you tell?
16. Now what did the little girl pray for?
17. How was the Christmas Promise fulfilled?

Copywork

> Ask and ye shall receive. For even the sparrow finds a home and the swallow a nest.
>
> —From *The Christmas Promise*

Parent's Help Page
(*The Christmas Promise*)

Observation

1. Study the hobo signs supplied inside the book's front and back covers.

2. Read the author's note at the beginning of the book. With your child discuss other forms of communication (cell phones, Internet, sign language) and how the hobos used hobo signs as a way of communication in an age when they didn't have the forms of communication we have today.

3. Discuss with your child the father and daughter's situation. Why would a parent have to leave a child in someone else's care? Was it the best thing for this child? Discuss the father's feelings. Discuss the child's feelings. Some children will be very sensitive to this book and the issues it raises so parents need to discern how much a child is prepared to understand and discuss.

Discussion Answers

1. The story begins in autumn.
2. The railroad bull's job was to keep people from trespassing into the rail yard and boxcars and getting a free ride. The little girl and her father snuck onto a boxcar because they had no money.
3. No. Discuss.
4. The father was looking for work to provide for his daughter.
5. Some of the danger hobos had to watch for were: lack of food, a safe place to sleep, mean dogs, the bitter cold, going to jail, being separated, having their clothes and shoes stolen. Listen to any other dangers your child might think of.
6. Hobos protected themselves from the cold by folding newspapers inside their coats and wrapping their shoes with tape.
7. They slept in the missions.
8. They tied their shoes around their wrists so nobody could take them while they slept.
9. The mission lady taught the little girl to pray (see copywork).
10. The little girl prayed for "someplace good."
11. The father signed two circles on his daughter's hand which meant "Don't give up."
12. On the curb was scratched the hobo sign for "kind lady."
13. Yes. She wanted to stay where the kind lady was and the kitchen "smelled warm and sugary like cookies" but she was worried about her Poppa.

14. Poppa promised that he would come back for her as soon as he found work.
15. Yes, she was and yes, it was. Let the child say how he can tell.
16. She prayed for her Poppa to "find someplace good" and "Come back for me."
17. Her Poppa came for her "before the first Christmas star came out."

Enrichment Activities

1. Give your child a piece of chalk. On the sidewalk or a concrete slab, allow them to draw the hobo signs and tell what each one means.

2. Another featured *Christmas Mosaic* book regarding the hobo lifestyle is *An Orange for Frankie* by Patricia Polacco.

3. While you are reading and baking put on a pot of Hobo Stew. There are many versions of this hearty stew. For some it is merely a stew in which to put all the leftover meats you have on hand. A recipe might read: Use any ingredients you have on hand (meats, can of vegetables, cut up potatoes). Brown the meat, then drain the fat. Add vegetables and any savory spices you like. Simmer until the vegetable and/or potatoes are done.

Hobo Stew

1. Camping version: For each person you want to feed cut a piece of heavy duty foil. In each sheet place a raw hamburger patty in the center, then put a piece of onion and bell pepper, tomatoes, and a few chunks of potatoes on top. Salt and pepper to taste. Wrap foil up around meat and veggies, and twist foil on top to close. Place them over the campfire or grill. (If baking at home, bake at 400 for about 30 minutes.)
(Courtesy Lake Ariel Boy Scout Troop 102)

2. Home-Cooked version:
    4 cloves garlic, diced
    2 peppers chopped
    1 onions, chopped
    Sauté in 1 T oil, 1 T butter, 1 t. Worcestershire Sauce, 1 t. dry mustard, 1 tsp of salt and pepper.
    Add 1 $\frac{1}{2}$ pounds cut up stew meat or hamburger. Toss with the onion/pepper mixture. Cook about 15-20 minutes, stirring occasionally.

    In a large kettle put one can tomato soup, 1 can tomato sauce, 1 soup-can of water, and 1$\frac{1}{2}$ soup-cans of milk. Add 4 chopped carrots, 5 diced potatoes, and 1 (more) chopped onion. Add the sautéed beef and pepper/onion mixture. Cook on low for 45 minutes-1 hour, or until the meat vegetables are cooked to the tenderness you like. This can be held all day in the crock pot

One Christmas Dawn
Written by Candice F. Ransom/ Illustrated by Peter Fiore
Published by BridgeWater Books (Troll Communications), 1996. (Out of print)

Vocabulary

limestone	quarry	trestle	inscribe	frazzled
huddled	boar	shoat	brittle	chuff
foreign	wither	holler	recollect	thaw

Discussion Questions

1. Where did the girl like to sit and wait for the train?
2. What were some of the signs it was going to be a hard winter?
3. Why couldn't Papa work at the quarry?
4. When did he tell them to expect him home?
5. What were the girls suppose to see if they visited the hogpen on Christmas Eve?
6. When the girl got out of bed and saw summertime outside, do you think she was dreaming?
7. What did Papa's clothes smell like?
8. What did the new doll represent to the girl?
9. What was the most important thing to the girls that Christmas morning?

Copywork

Days gone, but not forgotten.
—From *One Christmas Dawn*

Parent's Help Page
(*One Christmas Dawn*)

Observation

1. Go over these phrases with your child and discuss what is meant by each one.

   - "...the winter it was almost too cold for Christmas."
   - "...we were so far back in the hills, we had to break day with an ax."
   - "The mountain held us in, like hands."
   - "...a gravestone with no name."
   - "I broke a skin of ice on the water bucket."
   - "...we had to thaw our words by the fire before he could hear them!"
   - "The whole world stood motionless, frozen by the cold."
   - "The stars were brittle chips of ice."
   - "My breath chuffed in frosty puffs like steam from the train."
   - "...we raced through the diamond-bright cold to the house."
   - "Light chased the cold darkness clean from the sky."
   - "The world was touched with summer."
   - "I heard the whistle of the Bristol train, chugging through the holler like a promise."
   - "Cloudy dawn crept through the window."
   - "The mountains parted before me like hands unclasping."

2. Now go over the list and find all the figurative references that treat the mountain as a person.

3. Observe the page where the girl is in the darkened room looking out the bright window. Now turn the page to observe the brightly lit picture with the cabin standing in a summery field. How do the author and artist both startle us out of this wintry world by simply turning the page? With your child, compare and contrast the two pictures.

Discussion Answers

1. The girl liked to sit on a gravestone with the words "Gone but" carved on it.
2. Some of the signs of a hard winter were: squirrels frantically burying their acorns to the point of exhaustion and the wooly bear's narrow orange stripe.
3. Papa could no longer work at the quarry because it was too cold.
4. He told them to expect him home at Christmas time.
5. The girls were supposed to see their future husbands.
6. Allow your child to answer and explain why.
7. Papa's clothes smelt like sidewalks and stores.
8. The new doll represented the other side of the hills and that one day the girl would get to see the city herself.
9. The most important thing was that they were all together.

Enrichment Activities

1. Read the Author's Note at the back of book. There is much interesting information that you can share with your children.
2. Try playing the Old Granny Gobble game described in the author's note. Discuss with your children how different were the games in 1917 from the games children play today.
3. Make Oyster Stew. (For many it is traditional to make a fish dish on Christmas Eve.)

Oyster Stew
Contributed by Teresa Alvarez

> 1/2 cup butter
> 1 cup minced celery
> 3 tablespoons minced shallots
> 1 quart half-and-half cream
> 2 (12 ounce) containers fresh shucked oysters, undrained
> salt and ground black pepper to taste
> 1 pinch cayenne pepper or a dash of hot sauce, or to taste

Melt the butter in a large skillet over medium heat, and cook the celery and shallots until shallots are tender.

Pour half-and-half into a large pot over medium-high heat. Mix in the butter, celery, and shallot mixture. Stir continuously. When the mixture is almost boiling, (bubbles appear around the edge of the pan) pour the oysters and their liquid into the pot. Season with salt, pepper, and hot spice. Stir continuously until the oysters curl at the ends. When the oysters curl the stew is finished cooking; turn off the heat and serve.

Night Tree
Written by Eve Bunting/ Illustrated by Ted Rand
Published by Harcourt Children's Books, 1991.

Read the story from beginning to end the first time. Then open to the first picture of the family loading the pick-up truck outside their home. Go through the following questions. As you go through them and progress through the book, you can have your child create a nighttime picture adding pieces to it as they appear in the story. (See directions below.)

1. What time of day is it? (Nighttime) How can you tell? (Dark/ Lights in house showing/Full- moon)
2. What season is it? (Winter) How can you tell? (Trees are bare/Family is wearing coats and hats)
3. What holiday is it? (Christmas) How can you tell? (Christmas tree in window/Wreath on door/Lights on house)
4. Does the family live in the city? Or country? (Country) Where does your family live?
5. What is the family loading into the truck?

(Answers will vary. There are no right or wrong answers; let the child explore his imagination then tell him "Let's see...Turn the page.")

6. Does the family look happy?
7. Does this family look like our family? How are they the same? How are they different?
8. What are the other people doing in the picture? Your child will probably focus on the family in the truck. Have him observe the side streets with Christmas shoppers. Ask him what he would be shopping for if he were on that street looking in the shop windows.

131

9. Make a list of the trees mentioned on the next page. (oaks, alder, maples, pines, spruces and firs)
10. Would you like to walk through the woods in the cold and dark?
11. What secrets do you think lurk in the woods?
12. What is in the box that the family brings to the woods?
13. Why do you think the family is decorating the tree with food.
14. Why does the father turn off the lantern?
15. Why do you think the family does this as a yearly tradition?
16. How did the family share the spirit of Christmas with the wood's animals on Christmas day? How does this sharing care for God's creation?

Enrichment Activities

1. Plan to take your child on a nature walk outside with this list to see what trees are in your yard. Bring drawing paper and crayons to do bark rubbings then research the different types of trees on the Internet or in a nature book.

2. To make the nighttime picture, gather the following supplies:

   - a sheet of black construction paper
   - star stickers
   - yellow foam piece or construction paper circle (for the moon)
   - Easter grass (for the grassy terrain)
   - twigs (for barren trees)
   - deer picture cut from magazine or coloring book
   - green felt
   - dried nuts, beads, popcorn

   Have your child use these materials to duplicate the picture of the family seeing a deer. As you read the story add things to the picture, like star stickers when they see the stars near the end of the story. After finishing the story, place a green felt tree on your child's nighttime picture and let him decorate it with various seeds and red paint balls or beads for apples. Have your child add his moon piece "swinging lopsided on top" of his Christmas tree.

3. Everyone take turns measuring one another to see how tall they've grown this year.

4. Discuss how owls hunt in the night for their food. Owls are *carnivorous*. Ask your child if he knows what this means. (It means they eat meat). What food does an owl eat? (Mice, rabbits, frogs, birds) Does an owl have teeth? (No, an owl doesn't have teeth) So how does he eat his prey? (Swallows it whole or in large chunks) If you can get an owl pellet (you can order these online), now would be a good time to dissect one. If you find a picture of an owl in a magazine, cut it out and have your child add it to his nighttime picture.

5. Use any of the following recipes to create bird feeders for winter.

    A. Pine Cone Feeder
        Mix $\frac{1}{2}$ cup suet, lard, or vegetable shortening with 2 $\frac{1}{2}$ cups cornmeal or uncooked oats until well blended. Optional: add chopped up dried fruit, chopped nuts, and/or 1/4 cup finely chopped leftover meat (only in cold weather).

        Tie a string onto the top of a pine cone. Cover the pine cone with the fatty mixture (above), and roll the pine cone in seeds. Hang it from a tree branch.

    B. String Feeder
        String dried fruit, such as apples, cranberries, and apricot. Hang the string in a tree and watch the birds come.

    C. Bread Stick Feeder
        2 pkg refrigerated bread sticks
        4 eggs
        Bag of bird seed
        Cooking spray
        String or yarn

        Separate eggs and set aside egg white. Separate bread sticks and form each one into a log. Brush the bread sticks with egg white, covering all sides. Roll bread sticks in bird seed, covering entirely. Form the bread stick into a shape that can hang from the tree (like a pretzel, or a circle, or a heart). Bake for 15-20 on a greased baking sheet at 350. Cool. Hang in a tree outside.

A Reflection on Hanukkah

by Kathryn Faulkner

Every December while Christians are preparing for or celebrating the birth of the Light of the World, Jewish families celebrate Hanukkah, the Festival of Lights. Christians often light Advent candles to mark the approach of Christmas; Jews light candles to remember a miracle that took place 200 years before the birth of Jesus, when one day's supply of oil kept the lamp in the Temple of Jerusalem burning for eight days.

The lights illuminate our faith in God. While we do not know exactly when in the year Jesus was born, both Hanukkah and Christmas light up the darkest part of the year. The lights of the menorah shine out of Jewish windows to proclaim the miracle of Hanukkah just as the lights on our Christmas trees and Advent candles shine out of our windows to proclaim that the light of the world has come to guide us through the darkness. Although the candles celebrate two quite different events, there are some parallels and connections between our Christian faith and Judaism. Learning about Hanukkah, and about the Jewish faith as a whole, can help us to grow in our Christian faith.

Firstly, Jesus himself was a Jew, as were the disciples and many of the first Christians. It is likely that Jesus Himself would have celebrated Hanukkah by lighting candles or lamps. Although the miracle of the oil itself is not recorded in the Bible, the eight day celebration is mentioned in the book of Maccabees (see 1 Maccabees 4:56-59) and the lights of Hanukkah are mentioned by the first-century Jewish historian, Josephus. It is possible to imagine the Holy Family placing oil lamps in the window of their home in Nazareth.

Secondly, Jewish festivals often run parallel with Christian feasts, and we can see the Jewish year pointing the way the Christian one. The Crucifixion and Resurrection took place during the Jewish Passover, and Pentecost coincided with Shavuot, the Jewish Feast of Weeks. Hanukkah, like Passover and Succot (the Feast of Tabernacles or Booths), lasts for eight days. This is another Jewish tradition echoed in Christianity, where feasts of the Church year—in particular the great feasts of Christmas, Easter, and Pentecost—are also celebrated intensively for an "octave," or eight days.

Thirdly, the story of Hanukkah focuses on God's care for His people, particularly during times of trouble. He helped the Jewish people in their struggles against the Syrians, and He can help us in our struggles. As we look forward to celebrating the ultimate expression of God's care for us, the birth of His Son as a human baby, we can look back on the ways He demonstrated that care to the children of Israel. We come to appreciate the unwavering nature of God's love for us.

My husband is Jewish, so in our family we always observe Hanukkah both for his benefit and as a reminder to our children of their Jewish heritage. Although we have a special reason for appreciating Hanukkah, we also know that the celebration holds something for us as Christians, too. The festival reminds us that our faith is rooted in the Old Testament and characterized by God's care and protection for His people. The God of Abraham, Isaac, and Jacob is our God, too.

A Hanukkah Party

✶   Start by reading a Hanukkah story. You could read *Toby Belfer Never Had a Christmas Tree* or find another story at the library.

✶   Have a coloring competition. Many Hanukkah coloring pages are available on the internet.

✶   Light Hanukkah candles. The simplest way to do this would be to set out eight tea lights in a row. The candles are lit using a ninth, master candle called the *shamash*. Place this single candle behind the eight lights. It is easy to make a *menorah* using a strip of salt dough with nine candle holders set into it. The central holder is for the *shamash* and should be a little higher than the others.

✶   Play *dreidl*. A *dreidl* is a four sided spinner with a single Hebrew letter on each side. Each player starts with a pile of coins or chips (we use M & Ms). To start the game everyone puts two chips into a pot. They then take turns to spin the *dreidl* and act according to the letter that lands uppermost:

Gimel—Win everything in the pot. Each player then adds two chips each before continuing play
Hey—Take half of the pot
Nun—Do nothing
Shin—Add two chips to the pot.

Continue until everyone has played long enough or until all the chips are eaten!

✶   Make potato latkes:

Ingredients
4 large potatoes
3 tablespoons plain flour
$\frac{1}{2}$ teaspoon baking powder
1 teaspoon salt
2 eggs

Method
Peel and grate the potatoes. Drain off excess liquid. Beat the eggs. Add all the other ingredients to the potatoes and mix well. Heat oil in a skillet - I use oil about ¼ inch deep. Drop mixture into the pan by tablespoons and flatten slightly. Fry on both sides until brown. Drain on paper towels.

Latkes are traditionally served with apple sauce, and we like to eat them with salt beef.

✶   Serve donuts for dessert. Food cooked in oil is eaten as a reminder of the miracle of the lamp.

✶   End by giving everyone Hanukkah *gelt* (money). We always give each guest a bag of chocolate coins.

Toby Belfer Never Had a Christmas Tree
Written by Gloria Teles Pushker/ Illustrated by Judith Hierstein
Published by Pelican Publishing Co. Inc.., 1991.

Vocabulary
(Jewish definitions are easily found within the storybook)

Torah	latkas	menorah	shamash	universe
Sustain	dreidel	gelt	nations	insult
Sabbath	Ner Tamid	eternal	traditions	culture

Discussion Questions
1. What made Toby different from the other neighborhood children?
2. What had Toby never had that the other children had?
3. What was Grandmother's secret ingredient in her latkas recipe?
4. What was the prize for winning the game of dreidel?
5. What did Antiochus want all nations to bow to?
6. Did the Jews listen to him? Who did they bow to?
7. Instead of watching games, how did the Jews spend their time?
8. What would happen to a Jew found reading holy books and honoring the Sabbath?
9. Why did Jewish boys pretend to play a game of dreidel when the soldiers came around?
10. What miracle happened in the temple?
11. What is this miracle called?
12. What did the children in that town learn from Grandmother Belfer and Toby's party?

Copywork

Blessed art Thou, O Lord our God, King of the universe,
who commanded us to kindle the lights of Hanukkah. Amen.

Blessed art Thou, O Lord our God, King of the universe,
who has blessed our fathers and watched over them in the days of old.

Blessed art Thou, O Lord our God, King of the universe,
who gave us life, sustained us, and brought us to this happy season.
—"The Three Prayers" from *Toby Belfer*

Parent's Help Page
(*Toby Belfer Never had a Christmas Tree*)

Observation
Have your child narrate back to you the event that is known as "The Festival of Lights!"

Discussion Answers
1. Toby was the only Jewish kid in town.
2. Toby never had a Christmas tree.
3. Grandmother's secret recipe was matzo meal.
4. The prize for winning was chocolate money called gelt.
5. Antiochus wanted all nations to bow to his idols.
6. No, the Jews did not listen. They bowed only to God.
7. The Jews spent their time studying the Torah.
8. They were put to death.
9. So they would not get caught and be put to death.
10. The small amount of oil in the eternal light lasted for eight nights instead of just one.
11. This miracle is called "The Festival of Lights!"
12. The children learned about Jewish traditions and how nice it was to have a friend who could teach them about different cultures.

Enrichment Activity
At the back of the book, you will find a recipe for Potato Latkas, the rules for playing the game of Dreidel, and a guide for building a menorah. You and your child can enjoy doing one or all three of the activities.

~ Advent Week Four ~

Nativity
Epiphany
Angels

Sean Fitzpatrick

A Christmas Carol

Before the paling of the stars,
Before the winter morn,
Before the earliest cock-crow,
Jesus Christ was born:
Born in a stable,
Cradled in a manger,
In the world His Hands had made
Born a stranger.

Priest and King lay fast asleep
In Jerusalem,
Young and old lay fast asleep
In crowded Bethlehem:
Saint and angel, ox and ass,
Kept a watch together
Before the Christmas daybreak
In the winter weather.

Jesus on His mother's breast
In the stable cold,
Spotless Lamb of God was He,
Shepherd of the Fold:
Let us kneel with Mary Maid,
With Joseph bent and hoary,
With saint and angel, ox and ass,
To hail the King of Glory.
—CHRISTINA ROSSETTI

A Reflection on The Nativity

by Karen Edmisten

I remember when I first met Him—that Child who was born in Bethlehem. I didn't bump into Him during my childhood (though I now know He was there all along.) No, our first encounter—the one in which I was really a participant—came when I was older. I was a twenty-something atheist, and a friend recommended C. S. Lewis's *The Lion, the Witch and the Wardrobe* to me. "Pay special attention," he suggested, "to the character of Aslan."

My friend had a way of recommending things that dramatically changed my life, so I read the book. As urged, I "paid special attention" to Aslan, and I fell in love with him. And I fell in love with *Him*, though I still didn't fully understand Who it was that I loved. But I knew I wanted to hold Aslan forever in my arms and in my heart. Like Susan and Lucy, I wanted to bury my face in His mane, inhale His sweetness and never let go.

A few years later, the same friend gave me Barbara Robinson's *The Best Christmas Pageant Ever*, in which "awful old" Imogene Herdman, while playing Mary in the Christmas pageant, is walloped with the story of Jesus for the first time in her short, rough life. She can hardly bear the weight of the irony and the beauty. And as I read about little Imogene bawling her eyes out, I began to sob. I loved Imogene fiercely, and realized that I loved her because I *was* Imogene: I was that sad little girl who'd never known Jesus, but who one day collided headlong with the reality and power of Him. The God of the universe had bowled Imogene over and she would never be the same. Neither would I.

What changed the Herdmans, the Pevensies, and me? That child born in Bethlehem two millennia ago.

That *child*. It's hard to fathom, isn't it? A child, born in a stable, in poverty, to a virgin. A child raised in relative obscurity. A child who for many years was nothing more than a carpenter's son. A child.

The Christ Child set a Herdman sobbing, made perfectly sensible little British girls follow a lion for the rest of their lives, and He crumbled my unbelief.

Such is the power of our precious Jesus, and of the books written about Him. Although I wasn't raised on beautiful tales of our Lord, I know the compelling power of beautiful images and of the written word. I want to share with my own children everything I can about Him. I want to give them the gifts of picture books, chapter books, and the Bible. I want to introduce them to storytelling, fine art, and great music. I hope to lead them, through these things, to the Source of all that is good, and true, and beautiful. I pray my daughters will remember countless, sublime meetings with Him and will yearn to inhale His sweetness, the sweetness of that baby in a manger.

That baby was born for us. He lived and died for us.

He loves us so much.

Let's pay special attention.

The Christmas Bird
by Sallie Ketcham/ Illustrated by Stacey Schuett
Published by Augsburg Fortress, 2000.

Vocabulary

weary	drab	chaff	lowed	staves
embers	kindled	singe	lurch	pomegranate
herald	throb			

Discussion Questions

1. Why did the little bird stop at the stable?
2. The book does not say, but who is the couple and who is the baby?
3. What did the older shepherd offer the couple?
4. What did the little bird do to spark the fire?
5. What happened to the bird when it stopped beating the fire?
6. What did Mary mean when she told the bird, "Keep the morning sun over your brave left wing."?

Copywork

Are not two sparrows sold for a penny? And not one of them will fall to the ground without your Father's will. But even the hairs of your head are all numbered. Fear not, therefore; you are of more value than many sparrows.

—Matthew 10: 29-31

Parent's Help Page
(*The Christmas Bird*)

Observation

Observe the first full-color illustration of the book. Have your child pick out familiar points of interest: the shepherds in the field, the star, the bird, the city. What city is this illustration depicting? (Bethlehem) See if your child can tell which dwelling the Christ Child is in.

Discussion Answers

1. The little bird was very tired and cold and did not know the way south.
2. The couple is Mary and Joseph and the baby is Jesus.
3. The older shepherd gave his cloak to Mary and Joseph.
4. The little bird began to flap her wings towards the embers.
5. The bird's plain brown feathers turned a deep red.
6. She was telling the robin how to travel south.

Enrichment Activities

1. Locate a picture of a Robin Red-Breast in a book or on the Internet.

2. Study migration of the Robin Red-Breast. Let your child ponder the idea of how these birds know when to fly south. What tells them when to fly and where to go? You could possibly research this with your children.

3. Small children might like to learn these traditional childhood nursery rhymes. Look for the onomatopoeia (words that imitate a sound—for example, "Meeow") in the first poem. Both poems can be used as copywork (bordered with bird stickers) and memorized.

Little Robin Red Breast

Little Robin Red breast sat upon a tree,
Up went pussy cat and down went he;
Down came pussy, and away Robin ran;
Says little Robin Red breast, "Catch me if you can".
Little Robin Red breast jumped upon a wall,
Pussy cat jumped after him and almost got a fall;
Little Robin chirped and sang, and what did pussy say?
Pussy cat said, "Meeow!" and Robin jumped away.

The North Wind Doth Blow

The north wind doth blow,
And we shall have snow,
And what will poor robin do then,
Poor thing?
He'll sit in a barn,
And keep himself warm,
And hide his head under his wing,
Poor thing.

4. A picture to color:

The Christmas Donkey
Written and Illustrated by Gillian McClure
Published by Farrar Straus Giroux, 1993. (Out-of-Print)

Vocabulary

keen	bray	merchant	trudge	thistle	lunged
caress	trot	smug	dawdled	lowed	bleated
baaed	bolt	ravine	guffaw	snort	nipped

Discussion Questions
1. What was wrong with Arod the donkey?
2. Why did people have to travel?
3. Do we still pay taxes today?
4. How did they travel back then?
5. At the beginning of the book, Arod brays that "Only a king is good enough for me." What vice or fault is shown in this statement?
6. Who was the first traveler to buy a donkey from the donkey dealer?
7. What did he pay for his donkey?
8. Who was the second traveler to buy a donkey from the donkey dealer?
9. What did he pay for his donkey?
10. Who was the third traveler to buy Arod from the donkey dealer?
11. Why did the donkey dealer tell the couple that Arod was "...my best: keen-eyed and sure-footed, gentle and brave." Was he telling the truth?
12. What did he pay for his donkey?

13. Why did the donkey dealer give Arod to the poor carpenter?
14. How did God work His grace through Arod the donkey?
15. Arod tells Ebed that he "carried something more precious than any baker" and tells Obed that his charge was "worth a hundred wine merchants and all their wine." What did he carry that was more precious and worth more?
16. In the end, Arod did indeed carry a king on his back. Was he still prideful?
17. Do you think Arod was completely changed at the end of the story? How can you tell?

Copywork

A richer man than you will choose me. Only a king is good enough for me.
My king will come, a finer man than you'll ever be.
I carried something more precious than any baker.
My charge was worth a hundred wine merchants and all their wine.
—Arod the donkey in *The Christmas Donkey*

Parent's Help Page
(*The Christmas Donkey*)

Observation

1. Look at the picture of Mary in the doorway. Arod is bowing his head to her? Why do you think he is doing this when he doesn't know who she is? Notice the rays of light around her. How is the donkey dealer acting? Why is he acting this way towards Arod?
2. List the things Mary and Joseph come across on their journey and what Arod sees instead. List the virtues Joseph gives Arod after each encounter:
    A lion/patch of thistles—bravery
    A snake/a falling star—sharp eyes (keen-eyed)
    A ravine/a shining angel—sure-footed

Discussion Answers

1. Arod was "too wild and proud."
2. People had to go to the town of their birth to pay taxes.
3. Yes. You may want to explain why people have to pay taxes.
4. They traveled by donkey.
5. Arod is portraying the vice of pride.
6. The first traveler to buy a donkey was a rich baker.
7. He paid gold.
8. The second traveler was a wealthy wine merchant.
9. He paid silver.
10. The third traveler was a poor carpenter and his wife
11. The donkey dealer said that because he wanted them to buy Arod. No, he did not tell the truth.

12. He paid nothing.

13. The donkey dealer was glad to get rid of Arod.

14. On the journey Arod was being impatient, weary, selfish, and proud. God turned these vices (faults) into virtues (good things) through the patience, strength, giving, and kindness of the carpenter and his wife. Arod became "keen-eyed and sure-footed, gentle and brave."

15. Arod carried Jesus Christ, the King of Glory, on his back.

16. God did allow Arod to carry a king upon his back but He humbled Arod before his donkey friends and before the whole town so that Arod knew it was through God's glory and not his own that he was privileged and blessed.

17. No, Arod was not completely changed. He disrupts the other animals so that he can kneel in front of "his king." This shows us that we can also obtain all the virtues Arod did but we are still human and will still have faults to overcome.

Enrichment Activities

1. Find various Christmas cards depicting the Nativity and Mary and Joseph's journey from Nazareth into Bethlehem. Compare these pictures to the art work and scenes found in *The Christmas Donkey*. Your child might notice that most scenes show a desert setting in contrast to the book's setting. Which setting does your child prefer? Find a book at the library or go online and do an Internet search of the Nazareth/Bethlehem region and see what the landscape looks like.

2. Make a collage with the Christmas cards.

3. You may want to read *St. Francis and the Christmas Donkey* as a follow up to this book. Compare the two donkeys.

The Friendly Beasts

Jesus, our brother, kind and good
Was humbly born in a stable rude,
And the friendly beast around Him stood;
Jesus, our brother, kind and good.

"I," said the donkey, shaggy and brown,
"I carried His mother up hill and down;
I carried her safely to Bethlehem town;
I," said the donkey, shaggy and brown.

"I," said the cow, all white and red,
"I gave Him my manger for His bed;
I gave him my hay to pillow his head;
I," said the cow, all white and red.

"I," said the sheep with curly horn,
"I gave him my wool for His blanket warm;
He wore my coat on Christmas morn;
I," said the sheep with the curly horn.

"I," said the dove from the rafter high,
"Cooed Him to sleep, that He should not cry;
We cooed Him to sleep, my mate and I;
I," said the dove, from the rafters high.

Thus every beast by some good spell,
In the stable dark was glad to tell
Of the gift he gave Emmanuel,
The gift he gave Emmanuel.
                    —Traditional

The Christmas Bird
Written and Illustrated by Bernadette Watts
Published by North-South Books, 1996. (Out-of-Print)

Vocabulary

trudge   steep   guilty

Discussion Questions

1. What was Katya's favorite toy that she wanted to give the newborn king?
2. What else did Katya bring with her?
3. What happened to the bread?
4. What happened as Katya climbed the steep meadow?
5. What was wrong with the bird whistle?
6. Why did Katya feel shy upon entering the stable?
7. Then, with all her gifts gone, what feeling did Katya experience upon standing before the newborn King?
8. What happened when she gave the baby King her broken bird whistle?
9. What gift did the newborn King give Katya?

Copywork

What can I give Him,
Poor as I am?
If I were a shepherd
I would bring a lamb,
If I were a wise man
I would do my part,
Yet what I can I give Him,
Give my heart.

—from "In the Bleak Midwinter" by
Christina Rossetti

Parent's Help Page
(*The Christmas Bird*)

Observation

1. What do you have in your home that makes you happy?
2. Discuss why Katya's little bird whistle was so precious to her? Discuss the lifestyle of Katya compared to our lifestyles today.

Discussion Answers

1. Katya's favorite toy was a wooden bird whistle.
2. Katya also brought her cat and some bread.
3. The animals of the forest came to eat it.
4. Katya slipped and fell, dropping her wooden bird whistle.
5. The bird whistle would not make a sound.
6. Katya felt shy because she had nothing left to give the newborn King.
7. Standing before the King, Katya experienced only joy.
8. The baby's hands closed over the wooden bird and, when he opened his hands, the bird had come to life and was whistling.
9. The newborn King gave Katya the gift of her bird, song, and joy.

Enrichment Activities

1. This is an old Swedish folktale. It was originally entitled *Der Weihnachtsvogel.* Find Sweden on a map or globe.

2. Envision giving a beloved toy to the newborn King. Write about (or narrate) what happens when you present the toy to Him. Draw a picture of the toy you would give.

Mortimer's Christmas Manger

Written by Karma Wilson/ Illustrated by Jane Chapman
Published by Margaret K. McElderry Books, 2005.

Vocabulary

cramped	tidbits	ornaments	morsels
snuffle	scuttle	scamper	scurry

Discussion Questions

1. Where was Mortimer's house and why didn't he like it?
2. What did Mortimer spy that was new and wonderful?
3. What did Mortimer see that was better than the Christmas tree?
4. What was the house and who was in it?
5. Whose bed does Mortimer use to sleep in?
6. What story did Mortimer hear a man telling one night?
7. Why was Mortimer so touched that a tear rolled down his cheek?
8. What did Mortimer do?
9. What did he ask Jesus to do?
10. Did Jesus send him a home? What kind of home was it?

Copywork

Jesus, you were born to save the world. Perhaps you could also
 bring me a home?

—Mortimer to Jesus in
Mortimer's Christmas Manger

Parent's Help Page
(*Mortimer's Christmas Manger*)

Observation

1. Small children will enjoy looking at the colorful illustrations. What does your child see inside Mortimer's small dark hole? (Lego toys, a bug, torn paper, a spider, a marble, pipes)
2. On the second illustrated spread, how can you tell what time of year it is? (Someone is carrying a Santa doll)
3. See if you child can name all the nativity figures as Mortimer moves them in and out of the stable.

Discussion Answers

1. Mortimer's house was under the stairs and it was cold, cramped, and creepy.
2. Mortimer saw a lighted Christmas tree.
3. Mortimer saw a house just his size.
4. The house was the Christmas stable with the holy family and nativity figures inside it.
5. Mortimer uses baby Jesus' bed to sleep in.
6. Mortimer hears a man telling the story of the birth of Jesus.
7. Mortimer was touched that Christ was born into a world that did not have room for Him, and Mortimer had removed the baby statue from his stable home.
8. Mortimer moved all the statues back into the stable.
9. He asked Jesus to bring him a home.
10. Yes, He did. It was a gingerbread house.

Enrichment Activities

1. On the third illustrated spread, observe the Christmas cards hanging on the wall. You and your child can watch for these things in the Christmas cards you receive this year.
   - Snowmen
   - Dove
   - Christmas tree
   - Angels
   - Wisemen
2. This would be a good time to make a gingerbread house with your family. This is a wonderful tradition to begin. You can easily make one using graham crackers and a good stiff frosting for glue.
3. *Gingerbread Baby* by Jan Brett is an excellent companion book to read with this book.

*Father and Son: A Nativity Story**

Written by Geraldine McCaughrean/ Illustrated by Fabian Negrin

Vocabulary

roosted   brandished   acorn   planed   hewed

Discussion Questions
1. During which night does this story take place?
2. What clues help you to guess that it's Christmas?
3. How does Joseph feel as he thinks about taking care of Jesus as He grows up?
4. Does Joseph need to care for Jesus completely on his own? If not who will help him?
5. How does St. Joseph's thinking change by the end of the story?
6. For which "presents" is Joseph grateful?
7. What gift does St. Joseph decide to give to Jesus? Do you think this will be pleasing to God? Explain.

*Study Guide contributed by Gwen Wise

Copywork

My hands are strong, God knows. And everyone needs
an extra pair of hands from time to time.
—words to Jesus from Joseph in the book
Father and Son

Parent's Help Page
(*Father and Son*)

Observation

1. Feast your eyes on the colors in this book; they're so rich and bright. Note the colors the artist used to portray nighttime on the first page; they are the "cool" colors: blues, purple, many different greens. Contrast those with the "warm" pink, oranges, peaches and gold on the page where Jesus is sitting in a tree watching the sunrise. Looking at the two different pages, discuss why the artist chose those colors for each scene.
2. Look at the scene on the second page. Discuss how artists often create light around Baby Jesus and the manger. Ask the child why he thinks artists do this. Compare this Nativity scene with others, using other picture books and your Christmas cards.

Discussion Answers

1. The story takes place on Christmas night.
2. The angels have "roosted," the shepherds have "hurried back to their sheep," and the story opens in the "stable."
3. First, we can tell that St. Joseph is feeling disappointed that he could not find a place for the Holy Family to sleep. Because of Joseph's great humility, he then begins to wonder how he can teach and protect Jesus. He is "speechless;" his "heart quakes."
4. Joseph will receive all the graces needed to care for Jesus. On the last page we read: "and his God watched over him."
5. Reassured by God in his prayers St. Joseph gains greater and greater peace, until finally he is content to offer Jesus just what he has.
6. "This wife. This night. This happiness. This son."
7. He will give Jesus his hands. Let the child explain why this would be pleasing to God.

Enrichment Activity

1. Spend some time looking at a Bible Atlas. Find out where Nazareth and Bethlehem are. Then trace the journey of the Holy Family from Israel to Egypt and back again. Next, find their route from home to Jerusalem for the Passover when Jesus was twelve.
2. Make a Christmas gift to give to dad or grandpa. Have your child trace his hand onto a sheet of cardstock and cut it out. Have your child write one thing dad or grandpa does for him with his hands (for example: Your hands build warm campfires). Decorate by lacing contrasting colored yarn around the edges or outline with glitter.

The Trees Kneel At Christmas

By Maud Hart Lovelace
Published by ABDO and Daughters Publishing, 1951, 1979
Image reprinted by permission of the publisher.

Vocabulary

bazaars	Arabic	narghiles	solemn	mandolin
transparent	manufacture			

Discussion Questions

1. What does Grandmother call Christmas Eve?
2. According to Uncle Elias, when do the trees kneel?
3. Why do the trees kneel on Christmas Eve at midnight?
4. Have your child describe the relationship between Grandmother and Uncle Elias.
5. When do the people in Lebanon consider Christ's true birthday to be? Why?
6. What American tradition did the children hope their father would do again this Christmas?
7. What is some of the vegetation found in Lebanon?
8. What wonders happened in the village on the Night of the Birth?
9. What does Afify pray to see?
10. Why is Afify trying to act like a saint?
11. How is Arabic read as compared to the way Americans read?
12. Why do the relatives make Afify think of a flock of birds?

13. Was it a wise decision for the children to go to the park by themselves? What could have happened?
14. Do Afify and Hanna see the trees kneeling? How do you think they feel?

Copywork

> Faith is believing. It is knowing that God, our Creator, can do anything.
> —Grandmother in *The Trees Kneel at Christmas*

> It is easier to do something hard than it is to wait for the time to begin it.
> —Afify in *The Trees Kneel at Christmas*

> "Who am I," asked Uncle Elias, "to question how God chooses to perform His miracles?" And Uncle Elias blessed himself, too.
> —From *The Trees Kneel at Christmas*

Parent's Help Page
(*The Trees Kneel at Christmas*)

Observation
1. Discuss your favorite part of the book.
2. Study the painting of the street scene in Chapter 5. How does the artist portray Afify's confusion in the following paragraph from Chapter 5?

> But she felt her tears coming. When she opened her eyes, the spears of light thrown by the cars had fuzzy, golden edges. And the street lights had fuzzy diadems. She rubbed her eyes.

What does it mean that the street lights had diadems? Discuss the word "diadem."

Discussion Answers
1. Grandmother called Christmas Eve the "Night of the Birth."
2. Uncle Elias said the trees knelt on Epiphany Eve.
3. The trees bow on Christmas Eve because the Christ Child has come into the world and all creation bows to Him.
4. Have your child describe the relationship between Grandmother and Uncle Elias.
5. They consider the Lord's true birthday to be the day he was baptized because He was "born in the spirit."
6. They hoped he would buy a Christmas tree.

7. Some of the vegetation in Lebanon includes olive trees, fig trees, and mulberry trees.
8. On the "Night of the Birth" the church bells rang by themselves, all the waters are holy, all wild beasts become tame, and angels come down from heaven.
9. Afify prayed to see the trees kneel in her little Secret Place in Prospect Park.
10. Afify was trying to act like a saint because Grandmother seemed to think only saints saw the trees kneel at Christmastime.
11. Arabic is read right to left whereas English is read left to right.
12. The relatives "were so noisy and lively and bright."
13. Parents might want to point out the strange man the children met on the street and how Hanna could have gotten hit by a car.
14. Yes, Afify and Hanna saw the trees kneel. Let your child explain how he thinks they must feel.

Enrichment Activities

1. Have your child ask an older person who Hopalong Cassidy was. See if you can find a picture of him on the Internet.

2. Have your child find Lebanon on the map or globe and read aloud the first paragraph on page 23 which begins: "Lebanon was a land out of the Bible. ..."

3. Create a winter painting like the city street scene in Chapter 5 using crayon resist. Using nice art paper, (not construction paper), pencil-sketch the horizon line and landforms and/or buildings. Color the picture with crayon. Be sure the coloring is heavy so it will resist the paint. Leave some blank spaces where the paint will stick. Paint over the whole picture with thinned white tempera. (Experiment on a scrap paper first to be sure you have the thickness you like.)

4. Discuss Lebanese folkways with your child:
   - The people lived in small stone houses with flat roofs where people sat to talk, make lace, and smoke water-pipes.
   - They sat on the floor to eat.
   - The girls had gentler ways about them.
   - The beds were long cushions.
   - Everyone took their shoes off before entering the house.
   - The men kept their hats on inside.
   - It was considered better to have a boy first.

5. Discuss Lebanese food with your child:
   - Baklava—rich, sweet pastry (see recipe)
   - Leben—white cheese
   - Syrian Bread—thin round loaves like large pancakes
   - Halvah—candy
   - Turkish Coffee—black sweet, foamy on top-served in long-handled copper pot
   - Kibbee—a spiced patty of minced meats and bulgur (ground wheat)

- Eat & Be Grateful and Nest of a Bird—baklava-style pastries shaped like pies and doughnuts with nuts and honey.
- Yabra—grapevine leaves stuffed with rice and meat and white pine nuts.

5. Make a batch of baklava with your children.

Baklava
Contributed by Paula Soderberg

"My mother (Carole Laughary) said that her Mother (Evelyn Luta) and her Grandmother (Irene Gibeau) always made this for special occasions."

4 cups walnuts, finely chopped
$\frac{1}{2}$ cup sugar
1 teaspoon ground cinnamon
1 cup butter, melted
Honey, about a 12 ounce jar
1 pound Strudel leaves (phyllo)

Start early in the day. Grease 13x9 baking dish. In large bowl mix walnuts, sugar and cinnamon until blended - use a spoon, not a mixer.

Trim the phyllo into 13x9 rectangles. Place 1 sheet of phyllo in baking dish and brush with melted butter. Repeat 5 times so you have 6 layers of phyllo sheets. Sprinkle the last sheet with approx. 1 cup of the walnut mixture.

Now, place another sheet of phyllo over the walnut mixture and brush with butter. Repeat at least 5 times - you want to have at least 6 layers again. Sprinkle the last sheet with 1 cup of the nut mixture. Repeat this layering two more times.

Cover the last walnut layer with remaining phyllo and brush with butter.

Using a sharp knife, cut halfway through all the layers to make 24 servings. We usually do a triangle or diamond pattern.

Bake in 300 degree oven for 1 1/2 hours, or until top is golden brown.

Heat honey in a small saucepan over medium low heat until hot - not boiling. Spoon the hot honey over the Baklava. Cool the Baklava in the pan on a wire rack for 1 hour, then cover and just leave at room temperature until ready to serve.

To serve, finish cutting through the layers and place on paper doily on a small dinner plate.

A Reflection on Angels
"Do Not Be Afraid"
by Cay Gibson

Angels! How can we possibly think of Christmas without envisioning angels? Every year angels appear on our Christmas trees, sing upon our Christmas cards, and dance upon the pages of beautiful Christmas books. As messengers of God, they are forever connected with heralding in the Christmas season, bringing God's word and God's will to mankind.

As the Christmas season approaches, it is the perfect time to focus on what message the angels seek to impart to each one of us. To do that we must ask ourselves what the angels in Christmas stories tell us.

Let's look at the angels associated with that first Christmas and hear their messages.

The angel Gabriel spoke to Zechariah in his doubt: *"Do not be afraid, Zechariah,* because your prayer is heard, and your wife Elizabeth will bear you a son, and you shall call his name John. And you will have joy and gladness, and many will rejoice at his birth, for he will be great in the sight of the Lord" Luke 1:13-15.

Gabriel heralded the coming of Christ as man to the Jewish Virgin Mary: *"Do not be afraid, Mary,* for you have found favor with God. And behold, you will conceive in your womb and bear a son, and you shall call his name Jesus" Luke 1:30-31.

Then the angel of the Lord counseled Joseph: *"Joseph, son of David, do not fear* to take Mary your wife, for that which is conceived in her is of the Holy Spirit" Matthew 1:20.

These angelic beings announced the birth of a newborn King to humble shepherds in a field and the angel of the Lord reassured them: *"Be not afraid*; for behold, I bring you good news of a great joy which will come to all the people; for to you is born this day in the city of David a Savior, who is Christ and Lord" Luke 2:10-11.

Through these spiritual beings, God assures us of His protection and His provision. He rules us with the gentle, loving, hand of a child lifted above the straw in the presence of a simple family. He sends us His angels to guide us, protect us, and to make us aware that we have nothing to fear. *"Be not afraid,"* they assure us.

Because of the first Christmas, we, as Christians, need not be afraid because our God is greater than any plans we make (or don't make), greater than any unplanned pregnancies, greater than any earthly king, and greater than any army. He is greater than our own doubt and our own reservations. His has sent His angels to bid us: Do not be afraid.

And that is why the angels sing.

Bright Christmas: An Angel Remembers
Written by Andrew Clements/ Illustrated by Kate Kiesler
Published by Clarion Books, 1996.

Vocabulary

commandments   psalm   counselor

Discussion Questions
1. What were some of the names the Christmas child would be called?
2. Who was watching over Mary and Joseph when the innkeeper sent them away?
3. What was the one great truth that nothing could stop?
4. What song did the angels herald to the shepherds?
5. Who lit the path of the shepherds?
6. What is the happiest song that this angel says she ever sang?

Copywork

> And right now in the day in heaven,
> It is still that first Christmas night.
> —From *Bright Christmas: An Angel Remembers*

Parent's Help Page
(*Bright Christmas: An Angel Remembers*)

Observation

1. See how many amazing, beautiful, and important first things your child can rename that the angels brought to earth to prepare people for the coming of Christmas night:
   * Light and truth
   * Songs and messages

2. This book reads: "I have always been an angel...where I live there's really no time at all." Talk to your child about God and heaven not having a beginning and an end, how there are no calendars or clocks in heaven. Discuss how our life on earth revolves around a time schedule:
   * Getting up in the morning
   * Doing school work
   * Going to work
   * Scheduling doctor and dentist appointments
   * Meal times
   * Bed time
   * Birthdays, holidays, anniversaries

Discussion Answers

1. He would be called Prince of Peace, Wonderful, Counselor.
2. The angels were watching over Mary and Joseph.
3. The one great truth was the birth of Jesus Christ.
4. The angels sang: "Glory to God in the highest, and on earth peace, good will to men of good will."
5. The angels lit the path.
6. Christmas is the happiest song ever sung.

Enrichment Activity

1. See how often and where angels are mentioned in the Bible:

   * Angel guarding the entrance of the Garden of Eden—Genesis 3:23
   * Appeared to Abraham—Genesis 18:1-33
   * Jacob's Ladder—Genesis 28:12
   * Guardian Angels—Psalms 91:11, Matthew 18:10, Acts 12:15
   * Appeared to Daniel—Daniel 8:15-27
   * Appeared to St. John the Baptist's father—Luke 1:11-20
   * Appeared to the Virgin Mary—Luke 1:26-38
   * Counsels St. Joseph—Matthew 1:20-21
   * Angel to the Shepherds—Luke 2:14

- Talks to St. Joseph in his sleep—Matthew 2:13
- Comforts Christ—Luke 22:43
- Beholds the Face of God—Matthew 18:10
- Angels on the Day of Judgment—Matthew 13:49
- Stand Before God—Revelation 8:1-2

See if you can find any other passages in the Bible.

2. Discuss the various levels of angels:

First Hierarchy	Second Hierarchy	Third Hierarchy
Seraphim	Dominions	Principalities
Cherubim	Virtues	Archangels
Thrones	Powers	Angels

3. Use the angel pattern found in the Appendix to make angels to decorate your Christmas tree or mantelpiece. You may reinforce your discussion from #2 above and color code them for the hierarchies. Then place them on shelves in their hierarchical order.

Angels we have heard on high, sweetly singing o'er the plains
And the mountains in reply, echoing their joyous strains
Gloria, in excelsis Deo

The Holy Night by Correggio

A Reflection on the Epiphany

By Margot Davidson

A star more brilliant than the other stars arouses wise men that dwell in the far East, and from the brightness of the wondrous light these men, not unskilled in observing such things, appreciate the importance of the sign: this doubtless being brought about in their hearts by Divine inspiration, in order that the mystery of so great a sight might not be hid from them, and, what was an unusual appearance to their eyes, might not be obscure to their minds.

—From *Sermon 33: On the Epiphany* by Pope St. Leo the Great

Although most of us associate the word "epiphany" with the visit of the Magi to the baby Jesus, the word also conveys another meaning: It is used to express the moment when we make an intuitive realization, or something suddenly dawns on us. We get that "ah-ha" moment.

As an English teacher, I focus on fostering the right *atmosphere* in which a child can experience that "ah-ha" moment. There is nothing so delicious as that moment: the moment when we realize what is really going on in a story, when truth flares up suddenly in front of our eyes, or we see how the story relates to our own life and experiences. We discover what is underlying the story or realize something we previously didn't understand. It is not always a gradual unfolding; sometimes we are suddenly pierced with understanding and all the pieces fall into place. When something figurative is understood, when we hook the figurative to something real, that's when the epiphany happens. We say "Ah-ha," as we make the truth our own. The Wise Men experienced just such an epiphany and went in search of the truth they discovered.

As mothers, we are constantly creating an atmosphere in which our children can discover the beauty and wonder of the truth. We plan outings, we decorate the house with certain styles and colors, we select books and music—all in an effort to help our children discover the truths in the world and internalize them. We know that these truths will have so much more meaning to a child if he makes the discovery himself.

When it comes to Christmas, the creating of atmosphere intensifies. We decorate, we bake, we pray, we tell stories. We now want them to move from absorbing without realizing, to consciously seeing the connections and truths of our life in Christ. We want them to be pierced with understanding of the truth underlying the story of the baby and the stable and the Wise Men. So atmosphere abounds! We want them to realize Christ's enormous love for us: a love so enormous that it takes flesh, and from the Cradle smiles at the Cross; a love so big, it fills us and spills out of us into our desire to give to others. For children, it's not a big step. Their capacity for intuitive understanding is greater than ours. So we provide lots of atmosphere and they find the truth.

At the feast of the Epiphany, when Christ the King is made known to the world, we pray our children grasp the real meaning of the celebration. We plan and hope for an individual epiphany in each child's heart. We want each child to not only find the Child Jesus as the Wise Men did, but to be pierced with the understanding of what it *means* to find Him: "Ah-ha, this is true love—this is my life."

Star of the East

Star of the East, that long ago
Brought wise men on their way
Where, angels singing to and fro,
The Child of Bethlehem lay—
Above that Syrian hill afar
Thou shinest out to-night, O Star!

Star of the East, the night were drear
But for the tender grace
That with thy glory comes to cheer
Earth's loneliest, darkest place;
For by that charity we see
Where there is hope for all and me.

Star of the East! show us the way
In wisdom undefiled
To seek that manger out and lay
Our gifts before the Child—
To bring our hearts and offer them
Unto our King in Bethlehem!
—EUGENE FIELD

*Danny and the Kings**

Written by Susan Cooper/ Illustrated by Jos. A. Smith
Published by Margaret K. McElderry, 1993.

Vocabulary

rehearse	trailer	trudge	astonish
quarrelsome	café	parcel	snowbank
audience	drifts		

Discussion Questions

1. What did Danny want most of all?
2. What play were the children doing and what was Danny's part in it?
3. Why was Steve offering to get Danny a Christmas tree?
4. What happened to the tree?
5. Why was the truck driver frightened?
6. Who did Danny meet at the café?
7. What direction were the truckers driving? Why is this significant to the story?
8. What words were printed in the truck's cab over the Christmas lights?
9. What did Danny and Little Joe see on their way to the Christmas play?
10. Why was Danny upset after the play?
11. Why did his mother say that he was the best brother in the world?
12. What did they find in their trailer?
13. Where did it come from and what gives away the mystery?

*Image: *Adoration of the Magi* by Bartolomé Esteban Murillo

Copy Work

And going into the house they saw the child with Mary, his mother, and
they fell down and worshipped him. Then, opening their treasures,
they offered him gifts, gold, frankincense, and myrrh.

—Matthew 2:11

Parent's Help Page
(*Danny and the Kings*)

Discussion Answers
1. Danny wanted a Christmas tree for his little brother.
2. The children were performing the first Christmas and Danny was playing one of the three kings.
3. Steve felt bad about punching Danny.
4. The Christmas tree was damaged when the truck's wheels crushed it.
5. The truck driver was frightened because he feared he had hit Danny.
6. Danny met his neighbor, Luanne and two additional truck drivers.
7. The truckers were headed East which is significant because it was Christmas time and the three kings also traveled East in search of Jesus.
8. The words printed in the truck's cab were "King of the Road".
9. Danny's mother was worried about him.
10. Danny was upset because he had not been able to get his little brother a Christmas tree.
11. Danny's mother told his brother that he had "the best big brother in the world" because Danny had tried to make a happy Christmas for them.
12. They found a Christmas tree in their trailer.
13. The tree came from the three truckers. We know this because a red light bulb like those around the cab's windshield is found in the snow outside the door.

Observation
1. Have your child describe the truck's cab. Make sure your child takes special note of the Christmas lights hung around the windshield so he will recognize them at the end of the story.

2. Discuss the differences between travel today and what was available in Jesus' time.

Enrichment Activities
1. Are there any families that you know who have lost their husband/father and could use a Christmas tree this year?

2. Make Kings' Cake or Kings' Bread with your family. Hide a trinket inside the cake as a game for the children to play. Whoever finds it is "king" for the day. The recipe below for King's Ring gives directions for hiding a piece from the "dime store." You might consider hiding a little plastic baby Jesus or three small crowns. To integrate with the story you might hide three small trucks. You may just want to make a regular cake and frost and decorate it like a crown.

King's Ring
From *The Cook's Blessing* by Demetria Taylor
Random House, New York, 1965

$\frac{2}{3}$ cup milk
$\frac{3}{4}$ cup sugar
$1\frac{1}{4}$ t. salt
6 T shortening
2 pkgs active dry yeast
$\frac{2}{3}$ cup warm water (105°-115°)
3 eggs, beaten
7 cups all purpose flour
Melted butter, cinnamon-sugar mix
1 cup chopped Brazil nuts
1 cup mixed diced candied fruit

Scald milk, stir in sugar, salt, and shortening. Cool to lukewarm. Dissolve yeast in water; combine with lukewarm milk. Stir in eggs, then 3 cups of the flour. Beat until smooth. Stir in enough remaining flour to make a soft dough; knead until smooth and elastic. Put in a well-greased bowl; turn to bring grease side to top. Cover and let rise in a warm place until doubled. Punch down; turn out on a lightly floured board; divide in half. Roll each half into an oblong about 14 x 12 inches. Brush with melted butter and sprinkle generously with cinnamon-sugar. Combine Brazil nuts and mixed candied fruit; sprinkle one cup over each oblong. Wrap 2 dime store figurines in aluminum foil; tuck into the center of each oblong. Roll into 2 rope about $1\frac{1}{2}$ inches in diameter. Form each rope into a ring in greased 10-inch ring mold. Brush with melted butter. Cover, let rise until doubled—about an hour. Bake at 375° about 30 minutes. Cool on rack. Frost and decorate if desired.

The Holy Night

We sate among the stalls at Bethlehem;
The dumb kine from their fodder turning them,
Softened their horned faces
To almost human gazes
Toward the newly Born:
The simple shepherds from the star-lit brooks
Brought their visionary looks,
As yet in their astonied hearing rung
The strange sweet angel-tonge:
The magi of the East, in sandals worn,
Knelt reverent, sweeping round,
With long pale beards, their gifts upon the ground,
The incense, myrrh, and gold
These baby hands were impotent to hold:
So let all earthlies and celestials wait
Upon thy royal state.
Sleep, sleep, my kingly One!
                        —Elizabeth Barrett Browning

Celebrating December Birthdays

by Cay A. Gibson

"How lucky can you get?!"

"Wow, she'll get double the presents!"

"I wish I had the baby's birthday!"

Such were the sentiments of my children when they found out that our newest addition to the family was due on Christmas Eve 2001. They didn't see any down side to celebrating a birthday during the holiday season. They envisioned the confetti, the cake, the sparkling punch, and the merrily trimmed presents—twice as many as usual for their lucky sibling. They failed to appreciate that this busy time of year has little room for yet another party, that birthday presents and Christmas presents might well be one and the same, that family and friends might not be in town to help celebrate.

But if the kids had overlooked the problematic side of our Christmas delivery, the adults in my life who had been "Christmas babies" themselves felt compelled to share with me their sad stories of forgotten birthdays. Stories of being handed one gift and being told, "Here's your Christmas and birthday gift. Hope you enjoy it." Stories of birthdays being forgotten due to the Christmas hoopla. Stories of birthday gifts wrapped in Christmas wrapping paper.

Soon I was feeling sorry for this baby—even before her birth. I began to worry. Would she miss out on a day all her very own to celebrate? Would she feel deprived that she had to "share" the limelight with St. Nick and baby Jesus? It became my motherly mission to look for ideas to preplan future birthdays. I spoke to anyone I knew who had a December birthday and asked how I could best help my little one celebrate her day.

Then writer Elizabeth Foss reminded me that "A Baby at Christmas is what it's all about." I put my practical, analytical leanings aside and romanticized about the beauty of the season. I realized how amazing it would be to celebrate the birth of our Lord as I treasured my newborn babe. New life, new beginnings—isn't that what Christmas it all about?

So, with that insight fresh in my mind, I joyfully anticipated the challenge of making my little one's parties fun and creative—and of making her feel special. I embraced the task with the same eagerness and anticipation I had always shown for my other children's birthday celebrations. I decided that a December birthday would make for a very happy month!

As it turned out, Annie arrived before Christmas on December 20th. Today my most important goal is to make her special day *special* for her. It doesn't have to be loud or busy or crowded, but it must be as special, as unique, as she is.

List of December Do's.

- Emphasize the honor that this child shares a very special birthday month with the Christ child.
- Plan an indoor party in a room filled with balloons, confetti, streamers—and no trace of Christmas decorations.

- Wrap gifts in festive *birthday* wrapping paper.
- Make sure the birthday present is distinguished from the Christmas present—in other words, no "double duty" gifts.
- Put a birthday banner in a doorway of the house on the child's birthday.
- Save birthday/Christmas money and let the child go on a shopping spree at the Christmas sales.
- Remind the child that school is *closed* for the holidays.
- Always set aside a special time so that the child can open birthday presents from family members and friends.
- Let the child pick out birthday cake or help make it.
- Let the child select a theme for his or her party and go with that (something other than a Christmas-related theme).
- Give a special token birthday gift on the morning of birthday.
- Awake your birthday child with a special breakfast, complete with his or her favorite foods and a cup of hot cocoa topped with whipped cream!
- Before putting on the Christmas decorations on the tree, decorate it with streamers, noisemakers, and party favors!
- Consider celebrating a half-birthday party in June or July as an added treat for your Christmas baby.

The Rest of the Story . . .

Was I successful in making my daughter feel special on her holiday birthday? Well, perhaps I was too successful! One year, as we pulled into the church parking lot, my little daughter gleefully spotted the bright colorful lights on the sides of the church and squealed with delight at the huge Christmas wreath hanging from the rectory's bricked peak. She then clapped her hands as she proclaimed, "Mommy! Mommy! Everybody knows it's my birthday! Mine and Jesus'." That's when I realized that in all my efforts to emphasize the beauty of her birthday, I had conveyed to her the idea that *all* the lights, *all* the parties, *all* the decorations were for *her*. It was all about my little girl— and her best friend Jesus!.

So, in the end, it turns out that I should not have worried at all about my December baby. Annie loves her birthday. She loves her December celebration—the lights, the parties, the decorations, the beauty, the wonder, and the *specialness* of it all.

Books for December Babies to Read
Maggie Rose, Her Birthday Christmas by Ruth Sawyer
Silent Night by Will Moses
The Twenty-Four Days Before Christmas by Madeleine L'Engle/ Joe DeVelasco
Waiting for Noel: An Advent Story by Ann Dixon/ Mark Graham

Let it Snow
Mosaic Supplement

Here is an idea for a snowflake/winter reading discovery center that you can create in your home.

Make a snowflake winter reading table by gathering the items listed below and arranging them as described.

Items:

Nice-sized basket
Dishtowel with winter scene or snowflakes on it
Cut-out paper snowflakes
Pretty snowflake Christmas ornament
Film Negative
Camera
White packing foam pieces
Photo of Wilson Bentley in a frame copied from this site http://snowflakebentley.com/

Place the basket in center of a low table and line it with snowflake dishtowel. Hang snowflake Christmas ornament from basket's handle. Place paper snowflakes around basket and scatter white packing foam around basket. Place camera, film negative, and Bentley photo on side of basket. Place snow books around basket.

Snow Book Suggestions

Children of the Northlights by Ingri & Edgar D'Aulaire
Dear Rebecca, Winter is Here by Jean Craighead George/ Loretta Krupinski
First Snow by Kim Lewis
Geraldine's Big Snow by Holly Keller
Hannah's Bookmobile Christmas by Sally Derby/ Gabi Swiatkowska
Katy and the Big Snow by Virginia Lee Burton
Little Daughter of the Snow by Arthur Ransome/ Tom Bower
My Brother Loved Snowflakes by Mary Bahr / Laura Jacobsen (Fictionalized picture book of Bentley's, life similar to Snowflake Bentley, but from the brother's viewpoint. A well-done addition to *Snowflake Bentley*.)
Snow by Uri Shulevitz
Snow Crystals by W. A. Bentley and W. J. Humphreys (Wilson Bentley's catalog of his snowflake photos. Unbelievable! The first 20 pages give details of Bentley's life and work, but the 2400+ photos should prove quite interesting for the littles.)
Snow Riders Constance McGeorge/ Mary Whyte
Snowballs by Lois Ehlert
Snowflake Bentley by Jacqueline Briggs Martin / Mary Azarian
Snowmen at Night buy Caralyn Buehner/ Mark Buehner
Sugar Snow by Laura Ingalls Wilder/ Doris Ettlinger
The Big Snow by Berta & Elmer Hader
The First Snow by David Christiana

The Friendly Snowflake by M. Scott Peck / Christopher Peck (Problem with this book is it ventures a little into a new-age mentality on whether God is male or female and is reincarnation possible. Some families may want to avoid it. If edited, it's a great read about snowflakes and the wonders of God.)

The Snowflake - A Water Cycle Story by Neil Waldman (Month-by-month explanation of the water cycle.)

The Snowman by Raymond Briggs

The Snow Queen by Hans Christian Anderson / Susan Jeffers

The Snow Speaks by Nancy White Carlstrom / Jane Dyer

The Snowy Day by Ezra Jack Keats (also on DVD)

The Winter Noisy Book by Margaret Wise Brown / Charles G. Shaw

Too Many Mittens by Florence & Louis Slobodkin

Very Last First Time by Jan Andrews / Ian Wallace

When will it Snow by Bruce Hiscock

When Winter Comes by Nancy Van Laan/ Susan Gaber

White Snow, Bright Snow by Alvin Tresselt / Roger Duvoisin

Winter Holiday by Arthur Ransome

Poem Suggestions

Hut in Snow by Caspar David Friedrich

Snow Storm by Ralph Waldo Emerson

Stopping By Woods on a Snowy Evening by Robert Frost / Susan Jeffers

The Runaway by Robert Frost / Glenna Lang

Winter Poems by Barbara Rogasky /Trina Schart Hyman

Appendix

Crafts

AN ANGEL PATTERN TO CUT OUT

Color the angel, except on the area where it says PASTE. Turn the angel face down and bring the ends of her dress together in back. Paste one end to the other. When it is dry, stand the angel up and bend her slightly forward at the waist. To make the angel extra special, you can add cotton or angel hair to the wings.

For use with *Bright Christmas: An Angel Remembers.*

Kid-Friendly Ornaments

1. Doily Wrapped Ornament
    Materials needed for each ornament:
        12" round lace doily
        9" narrow ribbon or cording to hang ornament
        22" length of narrow ribbon (use several ribbons in different colors)
        Hot glue gun, other decorations, such as dried flowers, berries, miniature pinecones

Directions:
Insert cording into top of ornament and tie securely. Wrap doily around ornament and tie off with lengths of ribbon. Stretch doily over the ornaments and straighten the edges at the top. (Up to this point, this is an easy and fun ornament for children to make.) Add other decorations, if desired, attaching them with the hot glue gun. (Adapted from *Traditional Christmas Cooking, Crafts and Gifts*. Cy DeCosse, Inc., 1994)

2. Cinnamon Ornaments
   A. Salt dough cinnamon
        3 cups flour
        1 cup salt
        1 cup cinnamon
        1 cup nutmeg
        1- $2\frac{1}{2}$ cups of warm water

Mix dry ingredients in a large bowl. Add in the water a little at a time, mixing constantly until a soft dough is formed. Roll the dough to desired thickness and cut out shapes with a cookie cutter. Place ornaments on an ungreased baking sheet and use a straw to make holes for hanging the ornaments.

Bake for $1\frac{1}{2}$ hours at 225°. Place on a wire rack and return to the over for another $1\frac{1}{2}$ hours to ensure the ornaments are completely dry on the bottom. Decorate when cool.

   B. Applesauce Cinnamon
        4 oz. ground cinnamon
        1 tbsp. cloves
        1 tbsp. nutmeg
        2 tbsp. white school glue
        3/4 c. applesauce

Combine spices in a bowl, mix together. Add applesauce and glue. Work with hands until smooth. Mixture will be like wet dough, if too juicy add a little more

spice. Roll out to a 1/4 inch thickness. Cut with Christmas ornament indented cookie cutters. Cut a hole in upper edge of ornament with a drinking straw so ornament can be hung. Place on rack to air dry for several days (3 or 4 days), turning until dry. Do not put in oven.
(Recipe courtesy of Mrs. Kovaleski, 6th grade teacher, Sacred Heart School in Carbondale, PA)

C. Microwave Cinnamon Dough Ornaments
$2\frac{3}{4}$ cups flour
$\frac{3}{4}$ cup salt
$\frac{1}{4}$ cup ground cinnamon
1 T ground allspice
1 T ground cloves
$\frac{3}{4}$ t powdered alum
$1\frac{1}{4}$ cups water

Combine flour, salt, cinnamon, allspice, cloves, and alum in a bowl and whisk together. Add water and mix well to form a soft dough. Knead dough for 5-6 minutes, adding more flour if dough is too sticky or more water if too dry. Roll out to about $\frac{1}{4}$ inch thick and cut using cookie cutters. Decorate as desired with bits of whole spices or bits of dough attached to the main design using water. Use a straw to cut a hole in the top for the hanger. Spray a microwable dish with cooking spray. Place ornaments on dish and microwave for 5- 8 minutes on medium power, checking every few minutes and turning the ornaments to keep them from burning. Place on rack to cool and dry. After one day, attach the hanger. You can shellac them or spray with vegetable oil to make them look glossy.
(Recipe suggested by Terry Zuranski, adapted from *Traditional Christmas Cooking, Crafts and Gifts*. Cy DeCosse, Inc., 1994)

3. Cinnamon Stick Bundles
Glue a small stack of cinnamon sticks together. Tie a festive ribbon around the stack and hot glue decorations on the top.

4. Tinsel Filled Ornaments
(This can be used with any of the Christmas spider stories found in "Advent Week 1.") Purchase clear glass ball ornaments with a removable top. Remove the top and place tinsel of various colors in the ornament. Replace the top and string a ribbon or cording through the top and tie it off. Add decorations, if desired, to the top of the ornament.

NOTE: Clear glass or luminescent ball ornaments can be used in many ways. You can try putting a few drops of paint in and swirling the paint around in the ornament. Experiment with swirling additional colors.

5. Pine Cone Cinnamon Ornaments

Purchase or collect pinecones the size you want for ornaments or gift giving. Paint the pinecone "petals" with white glue. Generously sprinkle ground cinnamon on the "petals." Let dry for a day or two. Then shake off excess cinnamon. String a cord around the top to hang on a tree. Attach a festive bow at the top. (Alternatively, you can shake glitter on the pinecone after painting the glue on it.)

6. Jewelry Box Ornaments

Collect or purchase small cardboard jewelry boxes. (The boxes that earrings come in are just the right size.) You may also use small matchboxes. Wrap them like presents in colorful Christmas wrapping paper. Add ribbons and bows. Attach a hanger to them to hang on the tree or just place them on the branches.

7. 3-D Stars

Use heavy paper, such as cardstock. Trace two 5-pointed stars identical in size. Cut each one out and decorate as desired. Glitter pens are very nice for this! Cut a slit in one from an inside corner to the center. Cut a slit in the other from the tip of one point to the center. Slide the two together along the slits. This star can stand on a table or you can attach a hanger so that it hangs on the tree. You can make the pairs of stars in all different sizes and place them attractively with several different sizes in an arrangement on the mantle or table.

Recipes

The Christmas Pudding

Into the basin put the plums,
Stirabout, stirabout, stirabout!

Next the good white flour comes,
Stirabout, stirabout, stirabout!

Sugar and peel and eggs and spice,
Stirabout, stirabout, stirabout!

Mix them and fix them and cook them twice,
Stirabout, stirabout, stirabout!
—An English Traditional Poem
From *A Christmas Feast*, compiled by
Edna Barth, 1979

Index of Recipes in the Text

Index of Recipes in the Appendix

Basic Sugar Cookie

(For cut-out cookies)
Contributed by Margot Davidson
"This is a no-fail recipe that I have used for many, many years. For the best flavor, use real butter and real vanilla extract; it really makes a difference. Don't let them cook too long and get brown. We like them nice and soft!"

2 cups all purpose flour
$\frac{1}{4}$ t. salt
$\frac{3}{4}$ cup butter, softened
$\frac{3}{4}$ cup granulated sugar
1 large egg
1 t. pure vanilla extract
Frosting and decorations as desired

Combine the flour and salt and set aside. Cream the butter and sugar. Add the egg and the vanilla, beating until well mixed. Add flour and salt on low speed; do not overmix. Gather dough into a ball and flatten somewhat. Wrap tightly in plastic wrap and refrigerate for an hour until firm. (You can make this dough several days ahead of when you want to bake. Let the dough sit out for 10-15 minutes before trying to roll it.) On a floured counter or on a pastry cloth, roll the dough to about ¼ inch thickness. Cut with cookie cutters and place on an ungreased cookie sheet. Bake at 325°for 12-15 minutes. When cool keep in a plastic "ziplock" bag or some other airtight container. These freeze well also.

Padjeck (Potatoe Bread)

Contributed by Jen Salamon
"Here's a tradition from my husbands side that I have finally mastered! We serve this on Christmas Eve. The tradition, as far as I know, is Slovac. It's my husband's favorite food memory from Christmas Eve. It's so fulfilling to me, as his wife, to be able to make this for him. And he loves that I can make it for the kids. We listen to the story every year of how he would look forward to going to his grandmother's to eat the potato bread on Christmas Eve!"

1 loaf of frozen bread dough, thawed
Let rise and then roll out approx. 9x11

Filling:
4-5 boiled potatoes
1 cup cheddar or American cheese
Mix until smooth and cool

Place filling in center of bread dough. Seal up like a volcano, flip over, and flatten out. Bake at 350° for 30 minutes.

Cream Cheese Pastries

Contributed by Maria Cunningham
"These are very elegant!"

2 ½ cups flour
½ cup butter, softened
1 (8 oz) package cream cheese, softened
½ cup margarine, softened
¼ cup sugar
2 tsp. cinnamon
½ cup chopped pecans

Combine first 5 ingredients, mixing well. Cover and chill 24 hours. Divide dough into 4 equal portions. Turn each portion out onto a lightly floured surface and roll into a 12 in. circle. Sprinkle each circle with ½ tsp. cinnamon, 2 tbsp. sugar and 2 tbsp. pecans. Cut each circle into 12 wedges. Roll up each wedge starting at wide end. Place seam side down on greased baking sheets; Bake at 325° for 20 minutes. Cool. Yield: 4 dozen.

Panettone

Memory contributed by Maria Villa
Recipe by Margot Davidson

"This is an Italian sweet egg bread with dried fruits and raisins (sort of a fruitcake). My father is Peruvian and for some reason Panettone is traditionally eaten in Peru during Christmas.

We would buy it at the Latin grocery store, but now you can find it at most grocery stores. I can even find the Peruvian brands. I have fond memories of eyeing that trapezoid shaped box knowing that Christmas morning my father would open it up, unwrap the bread and cut out huge wedges for us that we would dip in our hot chocolate. And the aroma when he opened the box. Mmmmm."

$\frac{1}{3}$ cup warm water (105°-115°)
3 pkgs active dry yeast
3 t. sugar
3 eggs
$\frac{1}{4}$ cup sugar
1 t. vanilla
$\frac{1}{2}$ t. salt
$\frac{1}{2}$ cup butter, melted and cooled
3 cups flour, lightly packed
$\frac{1}{2}$ cup yellow raisins
$\frac{1}{2}$ cup dark raisins
$\frac{1}{2}$ cup candied fruit
Additional melted butter for brushing

Dissolve yeast in the water and 3 t. sugar. Set aside. In a large bowl beat together eggs, $\frac{1}{4}$cup sugar, vanilla, and salt. Add yeast and beat until well blended. Beat in melted butter and flour. Knead the dough until smooth and satiny. Shape into a ball and turn into a greased bowl. Cover and let rise in a warm place until doubled. Punch down and kneed in the raisins and candied fruit. Shape into a ball and place in a $1\frac{1}{2}$ quart soufflé pan (or a purchased Panettone pan) that is lightly greased and floured. Cover and let rise again until double.

With a knife indent the top with a cross. Brush top with melted butter and bake at 400° for 10 minutes. Reduce heat to 350° and bake for another 30 minutes or until top is deep golden brown. Cool in baking dish on a rack.

This bread dries out quickly because of the eggs, so be sure to eat it right away or keep it well wrapped.

(You can find more authentic recipes by searching online, but this one gives you the flavor with a recipe that is easier to manage. Most of the recipes are of Italian origin since it is a traditional Christmas bread in Italy as well.)

For an entertaining story about the origins of panettone, look for the picture book *Tony's Bread* by Tomie DePaola. It includes a recipe at the back.

Holiday Fruit Cookies
Contributed by Ana Braga-Henebry
From the Henebry Family cookbook

"One Christmas, my wonderful and loving mother-in law came to visit us and brought her recipes, per my request. I wanted my husband and children to enjoy the cookies she always makes for Christmas, cookies I did not grow up with. I grew up in Rio, Brazil! At Christmas, we have tropical fruit and gelatos. I learned from her, step by step, to make all sorts of Christmas treats.... and by the end of the most joyful Christmas season, I had a clear favorite. Here it is!"

2 eggs
3 $\frac{1}{2}$ c. flour
1 tsp. salt
1 tsp. baking soda
$\frac{1}{2}$ c. thick sour milk
1 $\frac{1}{2}$ c. pecans
1 $\frac{1}{2}$ c. candied cherries
1 $\frac{1}{2}$ c. dates

Combine the flour, salt, and baking soda in a bowl and set aside. Beat two eggs in a large bowl. Add the flour alternately with the sour milk to the egg, ending with flour. Add the pecans, candied cherries and dates with the last of the flour.

Bake at 400° for 10-13 minutes. Glaze with powdered sugar icing.

Three Favorite Cookies

Contributed by Jen Salamon

"I think of my mom every time I'm making these cookies with my children. We only make them in December to give out to friends and enjoy ourselves!"

Snickerdoodles

$\frac{1}{2}$ cup margarine or butter

1 $\frac{1}{2}$ c all-purpose flour

1 cup sugar

1 egg

$\frac{1}{2}$ t vanilla

$\frac{1}{4}$ t baking soda

$\frac{1}{4}$ t cream of tartar

2 T sugar

1 T ground cinnamon

In a mixing bowl beat margarine or butter with an electric mixer on med. to high sp. for 30 sec. Add about half of the flour, the 1 cup sugar, the egg, vanilla, baking soda, and cream of tartar. Beat till thoroughly combined. Beat in the remaining flour. Cover and chill 1 hr.

Shape dough into 1-inch balls. Combine the 2T sugar and cinnamon. Roll balls in mixture. Place two inches apart on an ungreased cookie sheet. Bake at 375° for 10-11 min. or until edges are golden. Cool on wire rack. Makes about 36.

Gingersnaps

2 $\frac{1}{4}$ C all-purpose flour

1 cup packed brown sugar

$\frac{3}{4}$ cup shortening or cooking oil

$\frac{1}{4}$ cup molasses

1 egg

1 t baking soda

1 t ground ginger

1 t ground cinnamon

$\frac{1}{2}$ t cloves

$\frac{1}{4}$ sugar

In a mixing bowl combine about half of the flour, the brown sugar, shortening, molasses, egg, baking soda, ginger, cinnamon, and cloves. Beat with an electric mixer on medium to high speed until thoroughly combined. Beat in remaining flour.

Shape dough into 1-inch balls. Roll in sugar. Place 2 inches apart on an ungreased baking sheet. Bake at 375° for 8 to 10 minutes or till set and tops are crackled. Cool on wire rack. Makes about 48.

Russian Tea Cakes (Sandies or Mexican Wedding cakes)
1 cup butter
2 $\frac{1}{2}$ cups all-purpose flour
$\frac{1}{3}$ cup sugar
1 t. vanilla
1 cup chopped pecans
1 cup sifted powdered sugar

In a mixing bowl beat butter with an electric mixer on medium to high speed for 30 sec. Add about half of the flour, the sugar, vanilla and 1T water. Beat till thoroughly combined. Beat in remaining flour. Stir in pecans.

Shape into 1 inch balls or 2 x 1/2 inch fingers or crescents. Place on an ungreased cookie sheet. Bake at 325° oven about 20 minutes or until bottoms are lightly browned. Cool cookies on a wire rack. Gently shake cooled cookies in a bag with powdered sugar. Makes about 36.

Fruitcake Cookies
Contributed by Lara Pennell

2 sticks butter
1 c brown sugar
3 eggs
3 c flour
1 t cinnamon
$\frac{1}{2}$ t baking soda
$\frac{1}{2}$ c sherry wine
1 t salt
2 T or more vanilla
7 c pecans
1 lb. candied pineapple
1 lb. candied cherries
1 lb. raisins
1 lb. dates

Blend butter and brown sugar. Mix adding eggs one at a time. Mix in cinnamon, soda, wine, salt, vanilla. Stir nuts and fruit with flour in a separate bowl. Mix with butter mixture. Make small cookies and bake at 300° 20-25 minutes and no longer. Makes 9-10 dozen.

Sugarplums

Contributed by Mary Gildersleeve
©2006 The King Arthur Flour Company, Inc.

These bite-sized treats have at least a 3-month shelf life at room temperature, well wrapped. Like fruitcake (which they resemble quite a bit in taste), they stay moist, soft, and flavorful for weeks. These are REALLY a great treat and not all that hard to make!

Fruit
10 ounces dried fruit, chopped (a scant 2 cups chopped)*
3 tablespoons brandy or rum

*Use just one favorite dried fruit, or an imaginative combination. We like cranberries, apricots, dried cherries or blueberries, and a touch of crystallized ginger.

Batter
$\frac{1}{4}$ cup (1/2 stick, 2 ounces) butter
$\frac{1}{2}$ cup (3 3/4 ounces) brown sugar
$\frac{1}{4}$ teaspoon salt
$\frac{1}{4}$ teaspoon ground cinnamon
$\frac{1}{8}$ teaspoon ground allspice or 1/4 teaspoon ground ginger
$\frac{1}{8}$ teaspoon ground nutmeg
$\frac{1}{4}$ teaspoon baking powder
1 large egg
$\frac{3}{4}$ cup (3 $\frac{1}{4}$ ounces) King Arthur Unbleached All-Purpose Flour
2 tablespoons (1 ounce) boiled cider*
2 tablespoons (1 $\frac{3}{8}$ ounces) light or dark corn syrup
$\frac{1}{2}$ cup chopped toasted pecans or walnuts**

*Or substitute an additional 2 tbs light or dark corn syrup.
**Toast nuts in a preheated 350°F oven for 8 to 10 minutes, until they're golden brown and smell roasted.

Coating
$\frac{1}{3}$ cup (2 $\frac{3}{8}$ ounces) extra-fine or superfine sugar
Chop the fruit fairly fine in a food processor. Combine with the liquor, cover, and let rest overnight. Or speed things up by microwaving the fruit and liquor (in a covered bowl) for about 1 minute, till the liquid is very hot. Leave the fruit covered, and let cool to room temperature.

Preheat the oven to 350°F. Lightly grease (or line with parchment) two baking sheets. Combine the butter, sugar, salt, spices, and baking powder, then beat in the egg, scraping the bowl. Add the flour, then the cider, syrup, fruit (with any remaining liquid), and nuts.

Drop the dough by teaspoonfuls (a teaspoon cookie scoop works well here) onto the prepared baking sheets. Bake for 12 minutes; the cookies will look soft, and will just be starting to brown on the bottom. Remove the cookies from the oven, and let them cool on the pan for 5 minutes. While the cookies are cooling, place the sugar in a medium-sized plastic bag.

While the cookies are still hot, gently squeeze them into balls. Place cookies in the bag, 6 or 8 at a time, and shake gently till they're coated with sugar. Place on a rack to cool. Store airtight. If you've stored cookies for awhile, shake with sugar again just before serving, if desired.

Yield: about 4 dozen 1" sugarplums.

Cranberry Nut Swirls

Original recipe by Jennifer Brockman

$\frac{1}{2}$ cup butter
$\frac{3}{4}$ cup sugar
1 egg
1 t. vanilla
$1\frac{1}{2}$ cups flour
$\frac{1}{4}$ t. baking powder
$\frac{1}{4}$ t. salt
$\frac{1}{2}$ cup cranberries, finely chopped
$\frac{1}{2}$ cup walnuts, finely chopped
1 t. grated orange peel
3 T. brown sugar
2 t. milk

In a mixing bowl, combine the bitter, sugar, egg and vanilla. Beat until fluffy, scraping the bowl occasionally. Combine the flour, baking powder, and salt. Add to creamed mixture. Refrigerate at least 1 hour. In a small bowl, combine cranberries, walnuts, and orange peel. Set aside.

On a lightly floured surface, roll dough into a 10-inch square. Combine brown sugar and milk and spread over the dough. Sprinkle with the cranberry mixture, leaving a ½ -inch edge at both ends of the dough. Roll up tightly, jelly roll style. Wrap with waxed paper and chill for several hours. Once chilled, cut roll into ¼ -inch slices and place on well greased cookie sheets. Bake at 375° for 14 minutes or until edges are light brown.
Makes 3 dozen cookies

Gingerbread Men . . . and Women

Contributed by Margot Davidson
"Another no-fail recipe that the kids love making every year."

$3\frac{1}{4}$ cups flour
$\frac{1}{2}$ tsp. baking soda
$\frac{1}{4}$ t. salt
1 t. cinnamon
2 tsp ginger
$\frac{1}{4}$ t. ground cloves
1 cup butter, softened
$\frac{3}{4}$ c. brown sugar (packed firmly)
1 large egg
$\frac{1}{2}$ cup molasses

Combine flour, soda, salt, cinnamon, ginger, and cloves in a bowl and set aside. Cream together butter and sugar. Add egg and molasses and beat until smooth. Add flour mixture slowly. Beat until just combined. Form dough into ball, flatten and wrap tightly in plastic. Refrigerate for at least an hour. (You can make this dough days ahead and keep in the refrigerator until ready to use it. If it's been refrigerated for a long time, let sit at room temperature for a few minutes before attempting to roll it out.) On a floured surface (counter, pastry cloth, or table), roll out to about $\frac{1}{4}$-inch thick. Using cookie cutters, cut out men and place on ungreased cookie sheet. Bake 10-12 minutes at 325°. Use frosting or decorate as desired.

Saint Lucy Buns

$\frac{1}{4}$ t. thread saffron, crushed
2 T boiling water
$3\frac{1}{2}$ - 4 cups all-purpose flour
1 pkg active dry yeast
$1\frac{1}{4}$ cups milk
$\frac{1}{2}$ cup butter
$\frac{1}{3}$ cup sugar
1 egg
Raisins
1 slightly beaten egg white

In a small bowl dissolve saffron in boiling water. In a large mixing bowl combine **2 cups** of the flour and the yeast. In a medium saucepan heat together milk, butter, sugar, and 1 teaspoon salt till just warm (115°-120°), and butter is almost melted; stir constantly. Add to flour mixture; add egg. Beat at low speed of electric mixer for ½ minute, scraping the sides of the bowl constantly. Beat 3 minutes at high speed.

Stir in as much of the remaining flour as you can mix in with a spoon. Turn out onto a lightly floured surface. Knead in enough of the remaining flour to make a moderately soft dough that is smooth and elastic (3 – 5 minutes). Shape into a ball. Place in a greased bowl; turn once to grease the top. Cover and let rise in a warm place till double (about 1½ hours).

Punch down, divide dough into quarters. Cover, let rest 10 minutes. Divide each quarter into 12 equal pieces. Roll each piece of dough into a 12 inch long rope. On a lightly greased baking sheet, form one rope into an "S" shape, coiling the ends snail fashion. (Figure 1) Repeat with remaining ropes. Make double buns if desired by pressing two of the S-shaped pieces together to form a cross. (Figure 2) Press one raisin into the center of each coil. (Figure 3) Cover and let rise until nearly double (40 minutes). Brush with beaten egg white and bake at 375° for 12- 15 minutes. Cool on a wire rack. Make 48 single or 24 double buns.

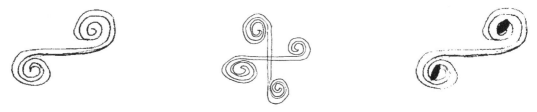

Figure 1   **Figure 2**   **Figure 3**

Saint Lucia Wreath

1 package active dry yeast
¼ C. warm water (105 to 115° F.)
¾ C. milk
½ C. (1 stick) butter, melted
1 t. saffron threads (a good pinch)
½ C. sugar
½ t. salt
½ C. currants
2 eggs, warmed
4 to 4 1/2 C. flour
1 large egg, beaten
Sugar sprinkles, optional

To make the dough: In a large bowl, sprinkle the yeast over the warm water. Add a pinch of sugar. Heat the milk and add the melted butter to it; cool until the mixture is lukewarm.

Pulverize the saffron with 1 teaspoon of the sugar, using a mortar and pestle or with the back of a spoon in a small dish. Add 1 tablespoon of the warm milk-and-butter mixture and allow the saffron to steep for 5 minutes.

Add the saffron mixture, milk-and-butter mixture, sugar, salt, currants and eggs to the yeast. Using an electric blender on medium speed, beat until blended. Add 2 cups flour and beat on medium speed for 2 minutes. Add 2 cups of the remaining flour and mix with a wooden spoon to make a medium-stiff dough. Let dough rest for 15 minutes.

Turn the dough out onto a lightly floured board. Knead for 8 minutes or until the dough is smooth and satiny. Place the dough in a clean, lightly oiled bowl. Turn the dough over to lightly oil the top. Cover and let rise in a warm place until doubled in size, about 1 hour.

To make a braided wreath: Punch the dough down and divide into 3 parts. With the palms of your hands, roll and shape each part into a rope-like strand about 36 inches long. Braid the strands by aligning them vertically and alternately crossing each outer strand over the center strand. Shape the braid into a circle and place on a greased or parchment-covered baking sheet. Pinch the ends together where they meet to seal the strands and to conceal the beginning and end of the braid.

Transfer to the baking sheet. Brush with the beaten egg. Sprinkle with sugar sprinkles if using. Let rise for about 45 minutes or just until puffy.

Preheat oven to 375° F. Bake for 20 to 25 minutes, until lightly browned, or until a wooden skewer inserted into the center of the dough comes out clean and dry. Cool on a rack. Makes 16 servings.

Note: To make two smaller wreaths: Divide the dough into 2 parts and braid as above. Place each wreath on a baking sheet, allow to rise and bake for about 20 minutes.
Source: *Scandinavian Feasts* by Beatrice Ojakangas (2001, University of Minnesota Press)

Embutido
Contributed by Stephanie Patag

"Embutido is one of our favorite Filipino dishes inherited from Spain. It is very similar to meatloaf, with some twists. Though it can be served year-round, it is certainly one of the highlights at the Filipino Christmas dinner table."

Maligayang Pasko at Manigong Bagong Taon (Merry Christmas and a Prosperous New Year, in Filipino)

3 pounds ground pork
1 large can vienna sausages, drained and pressed with a fork, or 1 cup finely chopped ham
1 chicken liver, sauteed in a bit of oil, and chopped finely, optional
1 cup grated cheddar, optional
$\frac{1}{4}$ cup bread crumbs
$\frac{3}{4}$ cup sweet pickle relish

$\frac{3}{4}$ cup raisins, chopped if desired

$\frac{3}{4}$ cup canned pimiento, or 1 large pre-roasted red bell pepper, chopped

3 eggs

2 teaspoons kosher or sea salt

1 tablespoon soy sauce

$1\frac{1}{2}$ teaspoons freshly ground black pepper

6 inches Spanish chorizo (not hot), Palacios brand recommended, or use Filipino canned chorizo (this comes packed in lard, and is available at the Filipino aisle of an Asian market), or 6 inches pepperoni, chopped, or quartered lengthwise (do not use Mexican spicy chorizo as it is a totally different product!)

$\frac{1}{2}$ cup pimiento-stuffed green olives, optional

2 hard boiled eggs, halved lengthwise

Water for steaming

Ketchup or homemade tomato sauce for serving

Equipment needed: large steamer or pot to fit the rolls

Set aside hard boiled egg halves, stuffed olives, and pepperoni if using quartered instead of chopped. Combine everything else in a large bowl. Use your hands to make sure you get a homogenous mixture. To test and see if your seasonings are right, take a small piece and shape into a patty, and fry in a dry skillet over low-medium heat for 5 minutes on each side or until done. Taste it and adjust seasonings as needed.

Divide mixture into two. On a flat surface form one portion into a large thick oval. Place the hard boiled egg halves in the middle, as well as the green olives, and quartered chorizo. Enclose the eggs, olives and chorizo in the meat mixture.

Embutido is traditionally cooked in muslin bags, the ends tied with string, so you end up with a round loaf. Some people choose to use aluminum foil for convenience. I personally don't like cooking in foil, so if I don't have muslin available I use parchment THEN foil—trickier to wrap but it works. Twist the ends firmly to enclose mixture. Steam the rolls in a large pot of boiling water, one hour. If you don't have a steamer, a pot will work fine; a clean folded up kitchen towel at the bottom and a plate can be used, or use a round metal rack.

Drain and chill until ready to serve. Cut crosswise into $\frac{1}{2}$-inch thick slices—you can make rounds or slice diagonally—and serve with ketchup or homemade tomato sauce.

Variations:
1. Use ground turkey, chicken, or a mixture of beef and pork.
2. The chorizo, olives and hard-boiled eggs can be omitted for a simpler dish. They are used for Christmas though, for a fancier presentation.
3. Chicken stock can be used in place of the water for steaming. The chicken stock is then reduced and mixed with ketchup or tomato sauce, and seasonings added to make a sauce for the sliced up embutido. Only do this when using muslin and not foil.

4. Embutido can be served at any temperature—cold, warm, hot, at room temperature. Cold slices are wonderful for a picnic or a deli buffet. They can also be sliced, pan-fried in a bit of oil, and served, napped with sauce.

5. Though the rolls can be served immediately, chilling makes them easier to slice.

6. If you don't want to fiddle with wrapping, these can also be cooked just like a Meatloaf—bake or steam as desired.

7. Sweet and sour sauce, bottled or homemade, is another option instead of the ketchup or tomato sauce. A brown mushroom gravy is also good!

8. One of the great things about this dish is that it can be made a couple of weeks ahead of time and frozen. Thaw in the refrigerator the day before you plan to serve.

A Typical, Untypical Australian Christmas Dinner
Contributed by Anna Hackett

"I come from an Italian background so these "untypical" recipes are not the norm for our family, but there have been Christmas's where we have embraced these delicious delicacies as a delightful change to our traditions."

Hors d'oeuvre
The ice-breaker course, especially if you have invited family and old friends. It is the conversational starter, the Christmas "spark" you might say!

Prawns and Avocado
These delectable "bites" are arranged so they resemble the babe in Mary's arms! Scoop balls of avocado flesh with a melon ball cutter. Marinate with shelled prawns in dressing, (2 teaspoons lemon juice. 2 tablespoons oil, salt pepper to taste). Cover and chill before serving, drain and insert a cocktail pick through the prawn and avocado. Thus having the prawn engulf the ball of avocado.

Almond Cheese Stars
These savoury biscuits keep well if stored in an airtight container, so may be made days before required. Here your conversation will focus on the star on that beautiful night!
8 oz. Cheese pastry (recipe below)
egg glaze
slivered almonds coarse salt.

On lightly floured board, roll out dough about ¼ inch thick. Using a star shaped cutter and put on ungreased oven tray. Brush with reserved egg-glaze, sprinkle with almonds and a pinch of coarse salt. Bake in moderately hot oven (375 F) for 15 minutes or until golden. Serve warm or cold.

Cheese Pastry
2 cups plain flour

2 tablespoons grated Parmesan cheese
4 oz. Butter
2 eggs
½ teaspoon salt
Sift flour and stir in Parmesan. Rub in the butter until mixture resembles breadcrumbs. Beat eggs and salt. Take out 1 tablespoon beaten egg, mix with 1 teaspoon water and set aside for glazing. Make well in centre of flour mixture and pour in remaining egg. Lightly mix to a smooth dough. Wrap and chill for at least 2 hours.

Cheese Straws
These bunches of "delicious" straw bundles will remind us of the Straw that Baby Jesus laid upon. And will decorate your table nicely!
3 oz. Butter
¾ cup finely grated Cheddar cheese
1 tablespoon grated Parmesan cheese
¾ cup plain flour
½ teaspoon paprika
pinch cayenne pepper
½ teaspoon salt
beaten egg

Cream butter and cheeses. Sift flour, paprika, cayenne and salt. Add to creamed mixture. Mix well, wrap in greaseproof paper and chill at least 1 hour. Roll out on lightly floured board to ¼ inch thickness. Cut into 4 inch lengths, then into ¼ inch wide strips. (For every 7 long straw bundle cut a wide strips to hug them into place, this makes the "bundles of cheese straws"). Put on baking trays, brush with egg glaze and bake in moderate oven (350 F) for 8-10 minutes. Cool on wire wracks and store in an airtight container.

First Course
Seafood is a light first course, especially in the hot summer of Australia. There are many ways to cook your seafood. The skewered "fritto misto" is a delightful dish served on a bed of salad and tangy lemon wedges!
1 lb scallops
1 lb raw shelled prawns
1 lb firm white fish
large stuffed olives
lemon wedges

Marinade
¼ cup olive oil
¼ cup of dry sherry
1 teaspoon grated fresh ginger
2 cloves garlic, crushed
1 teaspoon salt
freshly ground pepper

4 shallots, finely chopped

De- vein prawns, remove any dark portions of scallops,
But leave coral intact. Rinse quickly in cold in cold water and drain on paper towels.
Cover with marinade and leave at least 1 hour. Drain, reserving marinade. Thread
alternately on skewers, leaving a space between each. Put under preheated grill, brushing
frequently with marinade until lightly browned and cooked. Garnish with olives and
serve with lemon wedges.

Main Course

The Turkey is the "typical" for an Australian Christmas dinner. The only difference is
that we do not cook our turkey in the kitchen as the length of time it takes would heat our
home considerably! Instead it is cooked outside on a "weber", a sort of outdoor oven with
coals. Our other difference may be in the stuffing, this recipe is an old one of my mother-
in-laws.

Roast Turkey Sausage Stuffing:

1 ½ lb. Pork sausage meat
8 oz bacon rashers, diced
1 ½ cups diced celery
1 cup finely chopped onions
1 tablespoon chopped parsley
12 cups lightly packed soft breadcrumbs (homemade preferably)
3 eggs, lightly beaten
salt pepper.

In a frying pan over medium heat cook sausage meat, bacon, celery and onions together
for about 10 minutes or until sausage and bacon are cooked. Put with crumbs and parsley
into large bowl, add eggs, salt and pepper to taste and mix well. Wash turkey inside and
out and dry well. Spoon stuffing into neck cavity, stuffing into body.

As it is so warm, as a rule the turkey is served with potatoes usually cooked in the
"weber," too. Other vegetables accompanying the turkey could range from green beans,
eggplants, zucchini, garden fresh peas, and baby carrots. The list is endless. Salad
whether a crisp fresh salad or pasta salad, are also refreshing choices .

Dessert

Christmas dessert may include Frozen Christmas Pudding, Desert Christmas Pavlova
(recipe below), mince Pies, and an assortment of biscuits (cookies). And something our
children always look forward to: Homemade Christmas Ice-cream with an assortment of
exotic fruit.

Christmas Pavlova

"In Australia, during the Christmas season, fresh exotic fruit is available in abundance.
This is why " Christmas Dessert" would not be complete without the Christmas Pav!
Deliciously covered with luscious fruit!" Anna Hackett

6 egg whites
2 cups (12oz) castor sugar
1 ½ teaspoons vinegar
1 ½ teaspoons vanilla essence
icing sugar
1 punnet of strawberries, raspberries, blueberries, blackberries.
½ cup of passion fruit pulp sweetened
1 teaspoon Kirsch (optional)
Whipped cream.

If using a gas stove set oven at highest temperature just as you start to beat the egg whites. Beat egg whites at full speed until they stand in peaks. Sift sugar and gradually sprinkle 1 tablespoon at a time, beating at high speed only until all sugar has been added. Lastly, fold in vinegar and vanilla essence.

Draw a 7 inch circle on greased greaseproof paper or aluminum foil and put on oven slide. Heap egg white mixture on the circle on paper. Mould up the sides with spatula and make a slight depression on top to form a well-shaped meringue when cooked. Turn heat to lowest temperature just before putting Pavlova in bottom of oven to cook for 1 ½ hours. Remove from oven and leave until cold. When cool, spoon whipped cream high in the centre. Arrange ¾ of the strawberries, all blueberries, raspberries, and or blackberries, over cream. Crush remaining strawberries with a fork and press through a sieve. Sweeten with icing sugar and flavour with kirsch if desired. Pour this strawberry glaze over cream and serve .

NOTE: if using an electric oven, cook Pavlova at a low temperature (300 F) in the coolest part of the oven for 45-60 minutes, turn off heat and leave until oven is cold.

Coloring Pages

Epiphany

Flight into Egypt

Presentation, after a painting by Fra Bartolomeo

Presentation, after a painting by Titian

Nativity, after a painting by Lodovico

Mother and Child, after a painting by Raphael

Mother and Child, after a painting by Rucellai

Santa Adoring Baby Jesus

Epiphany
©Sean Fitzpatrick, Hillside Education 2007
Permission to photocopy for family use granted.

Saint Nicholas and Saint Nick
©Sean Fitzpatrick, Hillside Education 2007
Permission to photocopy for family use granted.

CPSIA information can be obtained
at www.ICGtesting.com
Printed in the USA
BVHW090026251119
564524BV00010B/138/P